Chuck and Blanche Johnson's Savor Cookbook™

Savor
Arizona
Cookbook

Arizona's Finest Restaurants
Their Recipes & Their Histories

Wilderness Adventures Press, Inc.™
Belgrade, Montana

© 2006 by Chuck and Blanche Johnson
Photographs contained herein © 2006 Blanche Johnson or as noted

Maps, book design, and cover design © 2006 Wilderness Adventures Press, Inc.™

Published by Wilderness Adventures Press, Inc.™
45 Buckskin Road
Belgrade, MT 59714
1-866-400-2012
Web site: www.wildadvpress.com
E-mail: books@wildadvpress.com
First Edition

Printed in Singapore

ISBN 9-781932-09827-3   (1-932098-27-5)

OTHER TITLES AVAILABLE IN THIS SERIES:

Savor Colorado
Savor Denver
Savor Idaho
Savor Montana
Savor Oregon
Savor Portland
Savor Seattle
Savor Wild Game

Table of Contents

— Chandler —

— Scottsdale —

— Paradise Valley —

— Phoenix —

The Grand View Trail, Grand Canyon circa 1906.

INTRODUCTION

Like so many of the western states, Arizona offers its residents and visitors an abundance of natural beauty and great opportunities for outdoor activities. The state is rich in history, with some of the most elaborate sites of ancient Indian cultures as well as many well-preserved sites depicting the westward expansion of settlers. Arizona has one of the most spectacular localities in the country for studying geologic history, in the Grand Canyon National Park. And, anyone who travels near the Tucson area is well advised to spend time at the Arizona Sonora Desert Museum, a fascinating display of all the flora and fauna that flourishes in the Sonora Desert along with detailed exhibits about the life process of the desert.

In the midst of all this natural splendor, both residents and tourists enjoy treating themselves to a lunch or dinner out at one of the many great restaurants in the state. As we traveled the state we were impressed with how many restaurants had designed their rooms to present the southwestern motif, and had placed windows and outdoor eating areas to maximize the views of the gorgeous geographic grandeur of Arizona. But, most importantly, we were truly impressed with the creative and innovative chefs in the state. There is a friendly spirit of competitiveness that keeps them at the top of their game while they also show a high degree of co-operation within a tightly woven culinary network. This culinary network is found in each state, but some of the chefs of Arizona have taken it to a new level with the organization known as the Tucson Originals, explained in this book along with its offspring, Dine Originals.

It is important to note that all of the featured restaurants were by invitation. None of the restaurants were charged for appearing in this book. We selected them based on the excellence and uniqueness of their food, as well as their ambience. Many have interesting histories. We also looked for places that feature comprehensive wine lists. We want to thank the owners, managers, chefs, and all the restaurant staff members who participated in getting this project to fruition.

The reader can use this book in several ways. As a travel guide, the reader can learn something about a restaurant's history, philosophy, and ambience, as well as the type of cuisine that it features. The map in the front gives the reader a perspective of the state and approximately where each restaurant is located. Since Arizona has a preponderance of restaurants in two locations, there are separate full-page maps of Phoenix/Scottsdale and Tucson to more accurately pinpoint locations.

Reading the recipes is a fun way to get a "taste" of each restaurant, and trying them out at home can be fun for the home chef as well as his or her guests.

Enjoy,

Blanche and Chuck Johnson

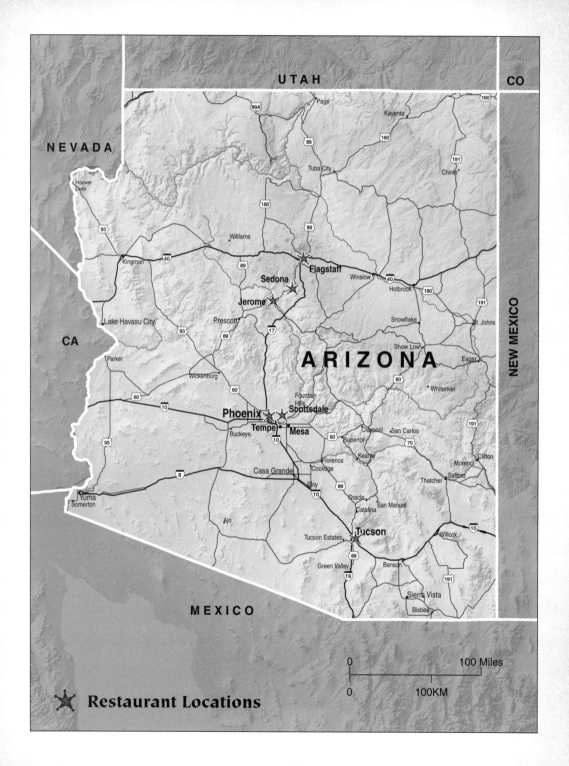

UTAH

CO

NEVADA

160

Page

Kayenta

89A

89

160

191

Tuba City

Chinle

Hoover
Dam

93

180

89

Williams

Flagstaff

40

Winslow

40

Kingman

89

Sedona

Holbrook

180

191

Jerome

CA

93

Prescott

17

Snowflake

St. Johns

Lake Havasu City

89

Show Low

ARIZONA

Parker

Eagar

60

Wickenburg

Whiteriver

60

Fountain
Hills

191

Phoenix

Scottsdale

Buckeye

95

60

10

Tempe

Mesa

Claypool

San Carlos

60

Superior

70

Clifton

Casa Grande

Florence
Coolidge

Kearny

Morenci

8

Eloy

89

10

Thatcher

Safford

Yuma
Somerton

Oracle

San Manuel

Ajo

Catalina

Tucson

Ajo

Tucson Estates

Willcox

10

89

Green Valley

Benson

19

191

Sierra Vista

MEXICO

Bisbee

NEW MEXICO

0   100 Miles

0   100KM

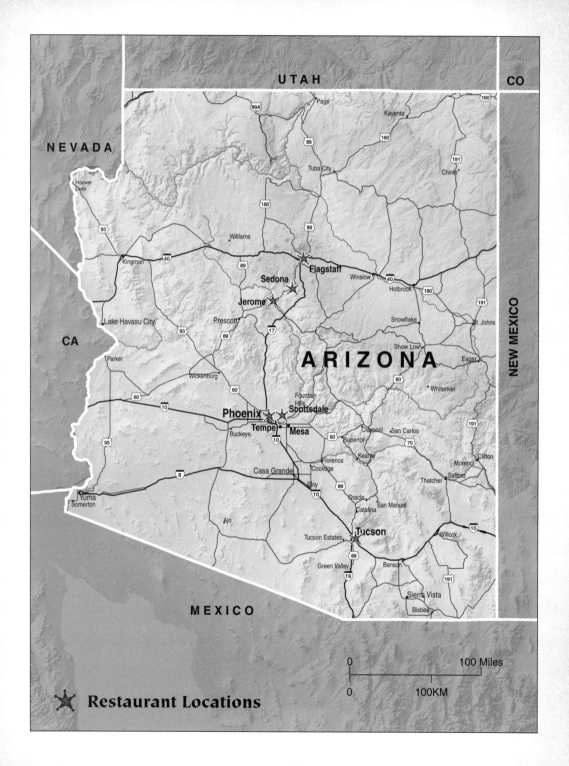 **Restaurant Locations**

SAVOR ARIZONA COOKBOOK
RESTAURANTS FEATURED

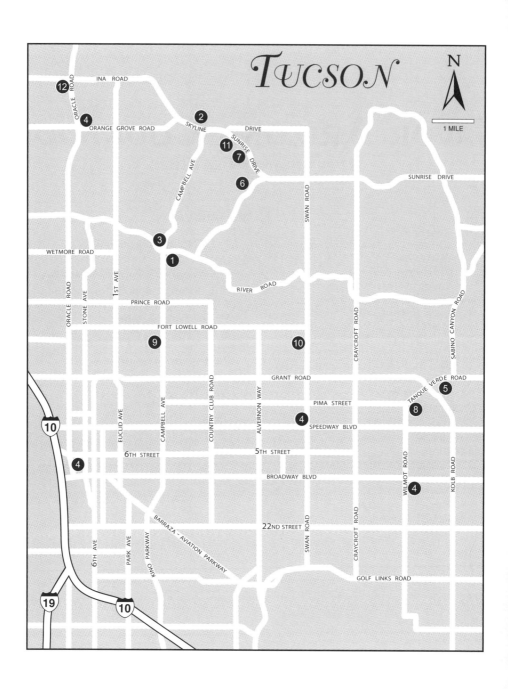

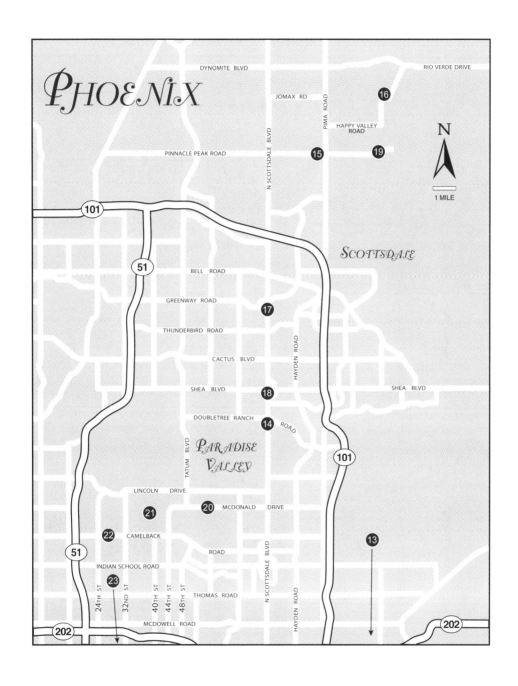

PHOENIX

DYNOMITE BLVD

RIO VERDE DRIVE

JOMAX RD

16

PIMA ROAD

HAPPY VALLEY ROAD

PINNACLE PEAK ROAD

N SCOTTSDALE BLVD

15

19

N

1 MILE

101

SCOTTSDALE

51

BELL ROAD

GREENWAY ROAD

17

THUNDERBIRD ROAD

HAYDEN ROAD

CACTUS BLVD

SHEA BLVD

18

SHEA BLVD

DOUBLETREE RANCH

14

ROAD

TATUM BLVD

PARADISE VALLEY

101

LINCOLN DRIVE

21

20

MCDONALD DRIVE

22

CAMELBACK

ROAD

51

13

INDIAN SCHOOL ROAD

N SCOTTSDALE BLVD

23

24TH ST

32ND ST

40TH ST

44TH ST

48TH ST

THOMAS ROAD

HAYDEN ROAD

202

MCDOWELL ROAD

202

Arizona Facts

Wyatt Earp (1848 – 1929) circa 1885.

Admission to Statehood:
February 14, 1912 (48th)
Sixth largest state in the union
114,006 square miles
310 miles east to west
400 miles north to south
Elevations - 70 feet to 12,633 feet
Counties - 15
Population (2002) - 5,456,453
21 Indian Reservations
27 State Parks
1 National Historic Park
2 Natioal Historic Sites
2 National Historic Trails
14 National Monuments
3 National Parks
6 National Forests
2 National Recreation Areas
1 National Memorial

Nickname:
Grand Canyon State
Primary Industries:
Manufacturing
Agriculture
Mining
Capital - Phoenix
Bird - Cactus Wren
Flower - Saguaro cactus blossom
(carnegiea gigantea)
Tree - Palo verde (cercidium)

Acacia
at St. Philips

4340 N. Campbell   **Open Daily at 11:00am**
Tucson, AZ 85718   **Sunday Jazz Brunch 11:00am to**
520-232-0101   **2:00pm**
www.acaciatucson.com

 # *Acacia at St. Philips*

Albert Hall, Chef/Owner
Lila Yamashiro, Owner
Dave Baker, Sous Chef
Yeny Grusenmeyer, Sous Chef

In November 2004, Chef Albert Hall and Lila Yamashiro opened Acacia at St. Philips, in the heart of the foothills region of Tucson. The restaurant was named after the species of hardy drought-resistant tree that comes in a many varieties. The restaurant offers an eclectic menu of Contemporary American Cuisine with hints of Latin and Pacific Rim as well as regional favorites lovingly hand-crafted for Tucson diners. According to Chef Albert Hall, American cuisine was actually the first fusion cuisine, since our country is made up of so many diverse nationalities that have added to the culinary melting pot.

With over thirty years experience in the culinary field, Chef Hall has traveled all over the country, absorbing many of these different cuisines. He received his first training at the Statler-Hilton in Washington, D.C. He then attended the prestigious Culinary Institute of America in New York and did his internship at the famous La Maisonette in Cincinnati. His culinary roots are classic French, modeled after the "cuisine rustique" of the French countryside. Albert's first job was with the 20th Century Rail Tours, a luxury rail trip from New York to Los Angeles that featured the regional cuisines of the states through which the train traveled, including Georgia, Mississippi, Louisiana, Texas, and Arizona. Two-day layovers were spent in New Orleans and in Tucson. Falling in love with Arizona, Albert first secured a position at the Arizona Biltmore, following that with chef positions at L'Auberge in Sedona, the Phoenician Resort, and five years at the exclusive Forest Highlands Golf Club in Flagstaff. While Chef at The Grill at Hacienda del Sol, Albert hired Dave Baker as a line cook. He also worked with Yeny Grusenmeyer who was serving her American Culinary Federation apprenticeship at The Grill. When Albert decided to open Acacia, both cooks came aboard as Sous Chefs. The other part of this team, Lila Yamashiro, impeccably runs the front of the house and serves as the stabilizing point for the entire crew.

Like the fusion menu, the restaurant is a blend of southwestern architecture with Asian influences. The clean lines of the interior are softened by the earth tones of the different woods and the tile floor, and accented by the soft teal of the upholstered bar chairs. The comfortable outside patio is a great place for a relaxing meal under the sycamores. Live jazz is a specialty of Acacia, featuring local artists on Fridays and Saturdays from 7:00pm to 10:00pm, and again during the very popular Sunday Brunch.

 Award of Excellence

Golden Tomato Gazpacho and Rock Shrimp Cocktail

The gazpacho is best if it is marinated overnight in the refrigerator.

Ingredients

¼ teaspoon salt
1 teaspoon pickling spice
8 ounces rock shrimp
1 teaspoon lemon juice
1 tablespoon olive oil
2 tablespoons lime juice
1 tablespoon cilantro, chopped

1 clove garlic, chopped
   Golden Tomato Gazpacho
    (recipe follows)
6 avocado fans
6 lime wedges to garnish
6 sprigs cilantro to garnish

Preparation

BOIL 1 quart of water and add the salt and pickling spice. Cook the shrimp for 2-3 minutes or until desired doneness. Remove the shrimp to an ice bath and chill until cold. Drain well, and then toss with the lemon juice, olive oil, lime juice, cilantro, and garlic. Marinate for at least 2 hours.

TO ASSEMBLE, chill martini glasses in the freezer for an hour prior to serving. Spoon the Golden Tomato Gazpacho into the chilled glasses. Float the marinated shrimp on the surface of the soup. Top with an avocado fan and garnish with a lime wedge and cilantro sprig.

Serves 6

Wine suggestion: Nobilo Sauvignon Blanc, Marlborough, New Zealand, 2005

For the Golden Tomato Gazpacho

½ cup English cucumber, puréed
4 golden beefsteak tomatoes, cut into
    ½-inch cubes
½ teaspoon garlic, chopped
½ kosher salt
1 dash cayenne pepper
¼ cup white balsamic vinegar
¼ cup extra virgin olive oil
½ cup orange juice
2 slices white bread, cubed

1 teaspoon sugar
1 yellow pepper, chopped
¼ cup red onion brunoise, cut ⅛ inch by
    ⅛ inch
¼ cup green pepper brunoise, cut ⅛ inch
    by ⅛ inch
¼ cup red pepper brunoise, cut ⅛ inch
    by ⅛ inch
1 tablespoon cilantro, chopped

COMBINE the cucumber purée, tomatoes, garlic, salt, cayenne, vinegar, olive oil, orange juice, white bread, sugar, and yellow pepper. Purée by batches in a blender for 1-2 minutes or until smooth. Add the red onions, green pepper, red pepper, and cilantro and mix well. Store this gazpacho covered in the refrigerator overnight before serving.

Brioche with Caramelized Shallots and Brie

Ingredients

½ pound Brie
    Brioche Dough (recipe follows)
1 ounce cream

4 egg yolks, beaten
    apple slices for serving

Preparation

HEAT oven to 350 degrees. Divide Brioche Dough into 3-ounce (by weight) portions and shape into rounds using the palm of your hand. Place the brioche in an oiled mold and place a 1-ounce cube of Brie (rind removed) in the middle of the dough. Push the Brie down into the dough. Roll a small ball of dough and place it over the cheese to seal it. Set the dough to rise a second time until it expands 75%. Make an egg wash with the cream and egg yolks, and brush it over the brioche. Bake for about 22 minutes. Serve warm with apple slices.

Yield: 8 brioches

Wine suggestion: Flora Springs "Soliloquy" Sauvignon Blanc, Napa Valley, 2004

For the Brioche Dough

¼ ounce instant yeast
¼ cup warm water
½ cup sugar
1 tablespoon salt
9 ounces milk, warmed
12 egg yolks, beaten

8 cups bread flour
1 pound unsalted butter, softened
8 shallots, peeled & trimmed
    olive oil
1 pinch sugar

HEAT oven to 400 degrees. Drizzle a little olive oil over the shallots and sprinkle a pinch of sugar over them, then toss to coat. Roast in the oven until caramelized. The shallots will break apart when cooked through. In a stainless steel bowl, mix together the yeast and ¼ cup warm water. When the yeast is dissolved, add the sugar and salt to form a syrup. Whisk in the warm milk and 12 beaten egg yolks. Transfer to a mixer fitted with a dough hook. Mix on medium speed and add the flour and softened butter in stages. This is sticky and very rich dough. Mix, scraping the bowl several times during the process. When the dough pulls away from the bowl, add the roasted shallots and mix just until incorporated into the dough. Turn the dough out onto a floured work surface and knead for 1 minute. Place the dough in a lightly oiled bowl and cover with a tea towel. Set to rise in a warm place for 1 hour, or until it has doubled in bulk. Punch down the dough and return it to the floured board. Knead it several times to homogenize the dough.

Roasted Tomato-Basil Soup

Ingredients

½ teaspoon garlic, chopped
1 small onion, diced fine
3 ounces butter
3 ounces flour
4 cups vegetable stock, heated
1½ pounds Roasted Tomatoes, roughly chopped (recipe follows)

5 leaves fresh basil, chopped
6 ounces heavy cream
salt and white pepper to taste
herbed goat cheese & toasted baguette, for garnish

Preparation

SAUTÉ the onions and garlic in butter until translucent. Add the flour and continue cooking on reduced heat for 5 minutes or until the roux has homogenized. Add the hot vegetable stock to the roux and whisk until smooth. Add the Roasted Tomatoes and basil, return to a simmer, and cook for 10 minutes. Then add the heavy cream and continue to cook for another 10 minutes. Season with salt and pepper to taste. Adjust the consistency with vegetable stock if it is too thick. Garnish with herbed goat cheese on a toasted baguette.

Serves 6

For the Roasted Tomatoes

2 pounds roma tomatoes, cored and cut lengthwise
1 tablespoon kosher salt

1 tablespoon granulated sugar
½ ounce olive oil

HEAT the oven to 275 degrees. Place the tomatoes on a sheet pan cut side up. Brush the exposed flesh liberally with olive oil, sprinkle with kosher salt and then with sugar. Roast in the oven for 1½ hours, or until the edges begin to turn brown. The tomatoes should have a shriveled look but remain moist inside. Remove them from the oven and let cool at room temperature. Store covered and refrigerated on a clean sheet pan until use.

ACHIOTE AND CITRUS CRUSTED LAMB RACK

Ingredients

14 ounces achiote paste
1 teaspoon garlic, chopped
1 teaspoon lemon rind, grated
1 teaspoon orange rind, grated
1 teaspoon lime rind, grated
2 lemons, juice from
2 oranges, juice from
2 limes, juice from

2 tablespoons Santa Cruz chili powder
2 tablespoons cumin seed, toasted and
  ground
2 tablespoons honey
1 teaspoon black pepper
  salt to taste
2 racks of lamb

Preparation

MIX the all ingredients except the lamb rack in a stainless steel bowl until a paste forms. Marinate the lamb in this mixture for 3 hours and remove. Scrape away the majority of the paste and pan sear the lamb on medium heat for 10-15 minutes, or until desired doneness. Baste it frequently. Remove it from the pan and slice between the bones. Serve immediately.

Serves 4

Wine suggestion: Steele Merlot, "Stymie Founders Reserve" Lake County, 2002

Acacia at St. Philips

Anthony's
in the Catalinas

ANTHONY'S
In the Catalinas

6440 North Campbell Ave.   Dinner served nightly
Tucson, AZ 85718   5:30pm to 10:00pm
520-299-1771   Lunch available for private parties
www.anthonysinthecatalinas.com

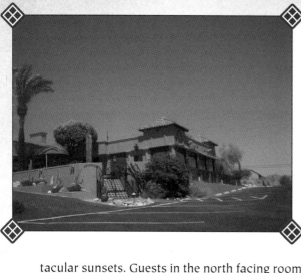

Anthony's in the Catalinas

Anthony and Brooke Martino, Owners

Nestled high at the base of the opulent Santa Catalina Mountains, Anthony's offers magnificent city and mountain views from its five dining rooms and outdoor areas. The room that faces southwest presents breathtaking views of the city of Tucson as well as spectacular sunsets. Guests in the north facing room are treated to beautiful views of the majestic Santa Catalina Mountains. Also available for groups of various sizes are The Wine Library, The Patio, and The Cellar, Arizona's only commercial underground wine cellar. Floor-to-ceiling arched windows look out onto patios that offer al fresco dining for many evenings, especially the spring and fall.

Owner Anthony Martino started in the restaurant business in 1965 as a busboy. Over the years, he worked his way up through the industry until he decided it was time to make a name for himself. He opened Anthony's in the Catalinas in 1989. Within a few years of opening, Anthony's had invested in an exceptional wine inventory that continues to grow and mature. In 1993, the *Wine Spectator* magazine awarded the restaurant the highly coveted *Grand Award*, which they have received every year since. This award is given to less than one hundred restaurants throughout the world. In order to qualify, a restaurant must have a minimum of 1,250 bottles of wine, with a serious depth of mature vintages, outstanding breadth in vertical offerings, excellent harmony with the menu, and superior organization and presentation.

The very attentive waitstaff at Anthony's is known for its impeccable service. The menu consists of Continental classics such as Chateaubriand and Duck a l'Orange con Confit Au Poivre. An Italian influence is deliciously presented in the Veal Catalina, a scaloppini of veal sautéed with artichokes, mushrooms, and scallions and served with a lemon beurre blanc. Also look for the Arizona touch in the Marinated Trio of Quail. The succulent game birds are stuffed with wild rice, golden raisins, sundried cranberries, and cipollini, with sautéed spinach and balsamic herb butter.

Along with the *Grand Award* for their wine list, Anthony's is also a consistent recipient of the AAA "Four Diamond" rating and the "DiRona" award from American Express. The restaurant has become a Tucson tradition, graciously hosting the many visitors to the area, as well as many locals who like to enjoy a special occasion dinner in a spectacular setting.

 Grand Award

MESQUITE GRILLED ASPARAGUS

Ingredients

28 spears asparagus
2 ounces prosciutto
2 cups balsamic vinegar
1 teaspoon cracked black pepper

2 teaspoons ancho honey butter
2 ounces goat cheese
2 ounces field greens
12 wedges roasted tomato

Preparation

GRILL the asparagus over mesquite until just cooked. Wrap with prosciutto and place in the center of the plate with the end of prosciutto on the bottom. Meanwhile, place the vinegar and pepper in a pot and bring it to a boil. Once the vinegar boils, reduce to a simmer and reduce the balsamic by half. Add the ancho honey butter and simmer for about 5 more minutes.

TO SERVE, drizzle the asparagus with the balsamic reduction sauce. Crumble goat cheese over the asparagus and garnish with a tuft of field greens and roasted tomato wedges.

Serves 4

SHRIMP LEJON

Ingredients

12 large shrimp, butterflied
⅛ cup horseradish
12 pieces uncooked smoked bacon

Rémoulade (recipe follows)
lemon and parsley to garnish

Preparation

HEAT oven to 350 degrees. Spoon the horseradish into the slit of the shrimp and wrap a piece of bacon around the entire shrimp, working from head to tail, and leaving the end of the tail unwrapped. Use toothpicks to hold the bacon in place. Bake (or fry) the shrimp to a deep golden brown, or until shrimp is thoroughly cooked.

TO SERVE, place 3 shrimp for each plate on top of the Rémoulade. Garnish with lemon and parsley.

Serves 4

Wine suggestion: Pinot Griggio "Jerman"

For the Rémoulade

3 tablespoons yellow onions, coarse
    chop
4 tablespoons capers, coarse chop
¼ cup pickles, coarse chop
¼ cup mayonnaise

⅛ cup sour cream
½ tablespoon lime juice
⅛ cup ketchup
1 teaspoon horseradish
⅛ teaspoon cayenne pepper

BLEND all ingredients well and chill.

CRAB CAKES

Ingredients

4 ounces backfin crabmeat
4 ounces lump crabmeat
2 tablespoons breadcrumbs
3 tablespoons mayonnaise
3 eggs

2 teaspoons Dijon mustard
1½ tablespoons horseradish
1¼ teaspoons parsley, finely chopped
1¼ teaspoons Old Bay seasoning
vegetable oil for cooking

Preparation

CLEAN the crabmeat of any shells, and then combine it with the breadcrumbs. Make a dressing with the mayonnaise, eggs, mustard, horseradish, parsley, and Old Bay seasoning. Pour the dressing over the crab and breadcrumbs, and mix by hand until all the ingredients have blended well. It may be necessary to add more eggs and seasonings if the crabmeat is particularly dry.

FORM into cakes and sauté in a skillet for approximately 5 minutes on each side, or until a nice, crisp golden brown.

Serves 4

Wine suggestion: Chardonnay "Neyers"

LAMB WELLINGTON WITH DIJON MUSTARD SAUCE

Ingredients

1 lamb loin, about ¾ pound
2 tablespoons canned duck pâté
8-10 mushrooms, chopped fine
1 tablespoon fresh or canned truffle, minced
2 shallots, minced
½ cup Madeira

2 6-inch squares of frozen puff pastry, thawed
2 large spinach leaves, blanched
1 egg yolk
1 tablespoon water
Dijon Mustard Sauce (recipe follows)

Preparation

CUT the lamb loin into 2 pieces and sear them all over in a hot skillet. Let the meat cool. For the duxelles, melt the duck pâté in a skillet and add the mushrooms, truffle, and shallots; cooking until the liquid from the mushrooms evaporates. Add the Madeira and deglaze the pan, then boil until the ingredients are almost dry.

HEAT the oven to 350 degrees. Spread the duxelles on the squares of puff pastry. Lay a spinach leaf on each one, then top with the lamb loins. Wrap up the loin and set the packages, seam side down, in a baking pan. Mix the egg and water together, and use this egg wash to brush the packages. Bake for 30 minutes for medium rare lamb, and serve with the Dijon Mustard Sauce.

Serves 2

Wine suggestion: Pinot Noir "Dymal"

For the Dijon Mustard Sauce

2 pounds lamb bones, browned in the oven
1 small yellow onion

1 clove garlic
salt and freshly ground pepper
Dijon mustard to taste

PUT the browned bones, onion, garlic, salt and pepper in a pot and cover the bones with about 5 cups of water. Simmer uncovered for 2 hours, and then strain out the solids and discard. Boil the strained stock until it has reduced to about ½ cup, skimming off the excess oil. Whisk in the Dijon mustard to taste, and reserve for serving.

Bistro Zin

ZIN BISTRO

1865 East River Road
Tucson, AZ 85718
520-299-7799
www.foxrc.com

Lunch Monday through Friday
11:30am – 3:00pm
Dinner Nightly 5:00pm – 11:30pm

 **Bistro Zin**

Christopher Cristiano, Executive Chef

O ne of Tucson's most enduring favorites, Bistro Zin is a French-inspired American bistro and wine bar. Honored as one of Tucson's Top Five Restaurants in the 2006 Tucson Lifestyle Culinary Awards, the restaurant has also won the magazine's awards for Best Bistro, Best Decadent Dessert, and Best Wine List. The restaurant has also won the esteemed Award of Excellence from the Wine Spectator magazine every year since 2002.

The emphasis on wine at Bistro Zin has resulted in an outstanding wine program. A cuvenet wine storage system allows over seventy different wines to be available by the glass daily, and includes an exceptional selection of wines that are usually only available by the bottle. A signature specialty of the restaurant is the program known as wine "flights", a tasting of three wines from different vintners that are related in style.

The innovative cuisine at Bistro Zin combines the rustic comfort food of European bistros with contemporary American techniques. The menu showcases outstanding dishes that change with the season in order to utilize fresh ingredients. The restaurant captures the ambiance and character of a traditional neighborhood bistro with its warm red tones and dark woods in both the dining room and the intimate bar. This ambiance is extended to the secluded climate-controlled patio with its fireplace and garden greenery.

Executive Chef, Christopher Cristiano, is responsible for the creative direction of Bistro Zin's menu, as well as all the other restaurants in the Fox Restaurant Concepts' stable of dining establishments. A graduate of the prestigious California Culinary Academy, he perfected his skills at some of the country's top restaurants, beginning in 1993 with an internship under Michel Richard at Citrus in Los Angeles. He worked with other culinary legends including Jean Francois Metaigner (the legendary chef of L'Orangerie) at La Cachette in Los Angeles and then on to Spago in Chicago, where he worked as roundsman for Wolfgang Puck. In 1996, Christopher returned to his hometown of Chicago where he worked with renowned chef Keith Luce at Spruce before turning his sights on Arizona. His energy and boundless enthusiasm for the work he loves has been rewarded with many favorable reviews and awards acknowledging the outstanding cuisine served at his restaurants. He loves the ongoing challenge of creating memorable dining experiences for his guests.

 Award of Excellence

SAUTÉED ARTICHOKES
with Black Truffles and Parmigiano Reggiano

This dish is for artichoke lovers. The mustard sauce really brings the rich flavors of this dish together and the truffles take it to new, delectable heights.

Ingredients

4 large artichokes
2 lemons, juice from
2 bay leaves
6 black peppercorns
    kosher salt to taste
    olive oil and butter to sauté
    Dijon mustard

balsamic vinegar, reduced to a syrup,
    to garnish
White truffle oil, to garnish
Chives, to garnish
1 oregano black truffle
    Parmigiano Reggiano

Preparation

SIMMER artichokes in water, lemon juice, bay leaves, peppercorns, and salt until the leaves are tender. Ice down the artichokes until they are cold, and then remove the leaves and quills. Slice the hearts thin. On medium heat, sauté the artichokes in olive oil and a little butter until golden brown. Add a tiny bit of Dijon mustard to lightly coat the hearts and continue to sauté until desired color is reached.

TO SERVE, place the balsamic reduction on a plate with drops of truffle oil and chives. Carefully place the artichokes in the center. Garnish with shaved black truffles and the Parmesan cheese.

Serves 4

MACARONI AND CHEESE

This recipe is a great time saver for working moms and anyone who wants to be able to prepare a delicious homemade meal in a very short time. The sauce may be made ahead of time and refrigerated. Reheat the desired quantity and mix it with the pasta as needed.

Ingredients

2 ounces extra virgin olive oil
1 medium onion, diced small
4 cloves garlic, sliced thin
2 bay leaves
1 quart half and half
8 ounces cream cheese
1 pound white cheddar cheese, grated
1 pound Swiss cheese, grated

8 ounces Gruyere cheese, grated
2 tablespoons kosher salt
1 teaspoon white pepper
3 pounds cooked pasta (bowties, penne, smaller types work best)
freshly grated Parmigiano Reggiano cheese to garnish

Preparation

IN OLIVE oil over low heat, sweat onion and garlic with the bay leaves until tender. Remove bay leaves, add the half and half and bring to a slow simmer. Gradually stir in cream cheese, white cheddar, Swiss, and Gruyere, beginning with the softest and ending with the Gruyere. Keep stirring until all the cheeses are melted and the mixture is smooth. Add salt and pepper to taste. Mix the sauce with the cooked pasta, and garnish with freshly grated Parmigiano Reggiano cheese.

Serves 12-15 as a side dish

LUMP CRAB WITH FIRE ROASTED CORN SALAD

This is a great summer dish, light and beautiful.

Ingredients

6 ears corn
1 cup Desert Glory tomatoes, quartered
¾ cup white balsamic vinegar
½ cup extra virgin olive oil
2 teaspoons kosher salt
1 teaspoon fresh cracked pepper
¼ cup chives, chopped

¼ cup cilantro, chopped
4-6 ounces pasteurized jumbo lump
    crabmeat
1 ounce fresh lemon juice
1 ounce white truffle oil
1 ounce parsley, chopped
1 pinch salt and pepper

Preparation

ROAST the corn in its husks on a grill, until it is golden brown. Let it cool, and then cut corn kernels off cobs. Mix tomato quarters with the corn. Toss with the vinegar, oil, salt, and pepper. Garnish with the chives and cilantro.

MIX the crabmeat, lemon juice, truffle oil, parsley, and salt and pepper. Place this crab mix on top of the corn salad and serve.

Serves 2

ROASTED DUCK WITH DRUNKEN CHERRY SAUCE

This is an elegant dish, perfect for special occasions.

Ingredients

1 ounce paprika
1 ounce herbs de Provence
½ ounce garlic powder
½ ounce onion powder
2 ounces black pepper

4 ounces kosher salt
*1 fresh duck, air dried for 24 hours in
   the refrigerator*
Drunken Cherry Sauce (recipe follows)

Preparation

HEAT the oven to 450 degrees. Mix the seasonings together. Generously rub the duck with the mixture, inside and out. Place the seasoned duck in the oven for 30 – 40 minutes, until well browned. Then reduce the oven temperature to 325 degrees and slow roast the duck for an additional 1½ hours. When the wing joint easily pulls away from the breast, the duck is ready. Serve with the Drunken Cherry Sauce.

Serves 2

For the Drunken Cherry Sauce

1 29-ounce can dark sweet cherries
2 tablespoons raspberry vinegar
1 tablespoon brandy
4 tablespoons port
2 tablespoons red wine

5 tablespoons sugar
4 tablespoons veal glacé
   *slurry of cornstarch and water mixed
      to consistency of cream*
   salt and pepper to taste

MIX the cherries and their juice, raspberry vinegar, brandy, port, and red wine in a large saucepan. Bring to a boil and then reduce it to a simmer. Mix in sugar with a wire whisk. Simmer for 15 minutes. Strain out the cherries and set them aside. Return the sauce to a simmer, add the veal glacé, and continue to simmer until the sauce begins to thicken, approximately 30 minutes. Add the cherry juice that has accumulated from the reserved cherries, along with a few tablespoons of slurry until the desired thickness is reached. Add the cherries back into the sauce and reheat. Salt and pepper to taste and reserve for serving.

El Charro Café

www.elcharrocafe.com

Downtown (The Original)	**North**
311 N. Court Ave.	100 W. Orange Grove
Tucson, AZ 85701	Tucson, AZ 85704
520-622-1922	520-615-1922
Eastside	**Speedway**
6310 E. Broadway Blvd.	4699 E. Speedway
Tucson, AZ 85710	Tucson, AZ 85712
520-745-1922	520-325-1922

www.elcharrocafe.com

Lunch and Dinner Served Daily

 **El Charro Café**

Carlotta Dunn Flores, Executive Chef/Owner
Ray Flores, Owner

Established in 1922, El Charro Café is America's oldest Mexican restaurant in continuous operation by the same family. Carlotta Dunn Flores' great-grandfather, Jules Flin, arrived in Tucson in the 1860s. A Frenchman and a master stones man, he had been hired to create the stone façade for Tucson's San Augustine Church. In 1884 he married Carlota Brunet, also of French stock. Their daughter, Monica, began El Charro Café, naming it after the romantic "gentlemen horsemen" known as los charros of Mexico. After living in Mexico for some years, Monica returned to Tucson on the death of her second husband. Borrowing money from a sister and with the culinary skills she had learned in childhood, she set up El Charro near a neighboring Chinese grocer, who served as her food purveyor for the meals she served in the narrow one-room restaurant.

With her business growing, Monica moved the restaurant two times before moving it to its present location on North Court Avenue in 1968. This was the location of the old family home that she had inherited. This home had been built by her father in the late 1890s and was part of the exclusive residential section of Tucson known as Snob Hollow. This section lay just outside the area that had encompassed the early Spanish presidio, and is designated as Site Number 14 in El Presidio District on the National Register of Historic Places. The high-ceilinged house is made of black volcanic basalt rock that Jules Flin had quarried from his claim at the foot of "A" Mountain, just west of downtown. Above the new entrance, Monica mounted her father's rifles that he had used to protect his family against Apaches.

During the 1940s, when many western films were being made in and around Tucson, El Charro was the favorite dining establishment of many of the Hollywood actors, producers, and directors, who were treated like family, including John Wayne and Ronald Reagan. In 1972, due to failing health, Monica let Carlotta Flores' mother, Zarina, take over the restaurant. Soon Carlotta and her husband, Ray, came on board with the goal of making the establishment more comfortable, and expanding the business, which now has four locations, as well as the catering business, Cocina Charro. Today, Carlotta and Ray are joined in the family endeavor with their daughter and two sons. One of Monica's favorite sayings was, "Whatever the meal, whatever the season, every meal at El Charro is served with color, music, and, whenever possible, good company."

TOSTADA GRANDE DE TUCSON

The custom is for each person to tear a piece from the tostada, although some people prefer to cut it into wedges, like pizza, before serving. A hot salsa, such as Salsa para Tacos, is usually spooned onto each bite.

Ingredients

1 18-inch flour tortilla
16 ounces longhorn cheese, shredded

Salsa para Tacos, optional
  (recipe follows)

Preparation

HEAT the oven to 400 degrees. Bake the tortilla for 5 minutes directly on the oven rack. Remove it from the oven and place on a pizza pan. Spread cheese evenly over the tortilla and bake it until the cheese is bubbly and completely melted, about 5 minutes. Cut into wedges and serve on a pizza tray or other round platter.

Serves 4 – 8 as an appetizer

For the Salsa para Tacos

1 16-ounce can crushed tomatoes
1 cup canned tomato purée, or substitute
    ½ cup tomato paste mixed with ½
    water
1 cup water
½ medium white onion, chopped

¼ cup garlic purée
½ cup oil
¼ cup vinegar
4 tablespoons dried leaf oregano
1 teaspoon salt, or to taste
4 de árbol chiles, optional

MIX all ingredients in a saucepan. Bring to a boil and turn off heat. Cool, taste, and adjust seasonings. Can be served hot or cold and can be stored in the refrigerator for up to 1 week.

Yield: 1 quart

CALDO DE QUESO (CHEESE AND POTATO SOUP)

Rough-cut potatoes and stringy cheese make this a soul-satisfier. Puréed and topped with a spoonful of tomato salsa, it is elegant. Caldo de Queso may be refrigerated for use the next day or frozen for later use.

Ingredients

4 medium potatoes, peeled and cubed
5 cups water
3 cups beef stock
1 teaspoon salt, or to taste
½ cup garlic purée (recipe follows)
8 fresh Anaheim chiles, roasted & chopped

1 medium white onion, sliced and separated
1¼ cups milk or evaporated milk
2 large tomatoes, coarsely chopped
4 cups longhorn cheese, cubed or shredded, or crumbled Mexican cheese

Preparation

IN AN 8-quart stockpot, cook the potatoes in water until soft. Remove the potatoes with a slotted spoon and set aside. Add beef stock to the potato water and bring it to a boil. Add salt, garlic purée, chiles, onion, and milk. Simmer for 10 minutes. Taste and adjust the seasoning, adding more chile if you like. Add cooked potatoes and tomatoes and simmer about 10 minutes.

TO SERVE, place ½ cup of the cheese in warm bowls and ladle the soup over the cheese.

Serves 6 – 8

For the Garlic Purée

4 heads of garlic   ¼ cup water

PEEL whole heads of garlic by smashing the cloves with the side of a wide knife. The peels will slip off easily. Put the peeled garlic in a blender with the water and purée. The purée should be about the consistency of applesauce. Store in a tightly closed glass jar in the refrigerator and use within a week.

Yield: ½ cup

Ejotes con Crema y Almendras

(String Beans with Cream and Almonds)

The basic idea of this recipe is adaptable to other vegetables and combinations: zucchini and red onion or chiles and yellow squash are good options.

Ingredients

1-1½ pounds fresh green beans, or 2 16-ounce cans French-style green beans

6 green onions

1 tablespoon olive oil or vegetable oil

¼ cup garlic purée
(see recipe in this section)

½ teaspoon salt
(omit if using feta cheese)

1 cup sour cream

½ cup Mexican or feta cheese, crumbled

½ teaspoon ground white pepper

½ cup slivered almonds

Preparation

IF USING fresh green beans, snap off the ends, string them if necessary, and slice lengthwise. Steam or boil until partially cooked and tender-crisp. Mince the green onion, reserving 1 tablespoon green tops for garnish.

IN A large skillet, heat oil and sauté green onion with garlic. Add beans and salt and sauté until warmed through. Add sour cream a little at a time, stirring carefully until the mixture is thick enough to coat the beans. Add crumbled cheese, stir, and adjust the seasoning.

TO SERVE, top individual servings with the reserved minced onion tops and slivered almonds.

Serves 6 – 8

Barbacoa (Barbecued Beef)

Ingredients

2 quarts water
3 pounds roast of beef (eye of round or brisket), cut into 12 pieces
¼ cup garlic purée

1¼ ounces pickling spice*, tied in a cheesecloth pouch
1 teaspoon salt
Barbecue Sauce (recipe follows)

Preparation

IN AN 8-quart stockpot, bring the water to a boil; add the meat, garlic purée, spice pouch, and salt. Bring to a boil again, skim the froth, and reduce the heat to a simmer. Simmer for 1 hour, or until the meat is tender, removing the froth as it accumulates. Remove the meat and let it cool enough to handle. Discard the spice pouch and reserve 1 cup of the cooking liquid to be used in the Barbecue Sauce. Shred the meat by pulling apart the fibers with your fingers. This meat will be added to the Barbecue Sauce. See recipe below.

HEAT the oven to 300 degrees. Place the seasoned meat in a large shallow baking pan and bake for about 1 hour, stirring occasionally.

Serves 6 – 8

NOTE: Pickling spice is available commercially, in a jar or box, but you can make your own easily. To make your own bouquet garni, combine the following in a cheesecloth pouch: cloves, cinnamon stick pieces, whole coriander seed, bay leaf, peppercorns, and other whole spices or herbs that appeal to you.

For the Barbecue Sauce

4 tablespoons oil
½ cup fresh Anaheim chiles, roasted & chopped
1 white onion, chopped
¼ cup garlic purée
1 tablespoon vinegar
1 cup reserved meat broth
1 8-ounce can jalapeños, drained and thinly sliced
1 tablespoon juice from canned jalapeños

1 bay leaf
cooked and shredded meat, see above
½ cup Salsa de Chile Colorado (see recipe under El Charro Frijoles Refritos)
1 teaspoon ground black pepper
½ cup green olives minced
4 large tomatoes, chopped
½ cup wine

IN A large skillet, heat the oil and sauté the chiles, onion, garlic purée, vinegar, broth, jalapeño, and jalapeño juice. Add the bay leaf, shredded meat, Salsa de Chile Colorado, pepper, olives, tomatoes, and wine. Simmer about 10 minutes, then remove the bay leaf and discard.

FLAN (CARAMEL CUSTARD)

This custard is rich, smooth, and delicious. We like to add a garnish, but you can serve it unadorned as well.

Ingredients

¾ cup sugar, divided
6 eggs, lightly beaten
1 pinch salt
1 teaspoon vanilla extract

1 quart scalded milk
whipped cream to garnish
Kahlua liqueur to garnish
slivered almonds to garnish

Preparation

CARAMELIZE ½ cup of the sugar by heating it in a skillet over very low heat, stirring constantly while it melts and turns brown. Do not cook past this point or it will harden into amber glass! Pour the caramel into individual custard cups or pour it into a 6-cup, shallow baking dish. Set aside.

HEAT the oven to 350 degrees. Combine the beaten eggs, the remaining ¼ cup of sugar, salt, and vanilla, beating well with a whisk. Stir in the scalded milk. Strain into the baking dish or cups over the caramel. Place the baking dish or cups in a roasting pan and add enough hot water in the roasting pan to come halfway up the sides of the baking dish. Bake for 20 – 30 minutes. Insert a knife into the center of the custard, and if it comes out clean then the custard is set. Cool and chill before serving. Garnish with whipped cream, a dash of Kahlua, and almonds, and serve.

Serves 8 – 12

THE WINE SPECTATOR AWARD

Many of the restaurants included in this cookbook have been recognized by Wine Spectator, the world's most popular wine magazine. It reviews more than 10,000 wines each year and covers travel, fine dining and the lifestyle of wine for novices and connoisseurs alike. Through its Restaurant Awards program, the magazine recognizes restaurants around the world that offer distinguished wine lists.

Awards are given in three tiers. In 2003, more than 3,600 restaurants earned wine list awards. To qualify, wine lists must provide vintages and appellations for all selections. The overall presentation and appearance of the list are also important. Once past these initial requirements, lists are then judged for one of three awards: the Award of Excellence, the Best of Award of Excellence, and the Grand Award.

- Award of Excellence—The basic Award of Excellence recognizes restaurants with lists that offer a well-chosen selection of quality producers, along with a thematic match to the menu in both price and style.

- Best of Award of Excellence—The second-tier Best of Award of Excellence was created to give special recognition to those restaurants that exceed the requirements of the basic category. These lists must display vintage depth, including vertical offerings of several top wines, as well as excellent breadth from major wine growing regions.

- Grand Award—The highest award, the Grand Award, is given to those restaurants that show an uncompromising, passionate devotion to quality. These lists show serious depth of mature vintages, outstanding breadth in their vertical offerings, excellent harmony with the menu, and superior organization and presentation. In 2003, only 89 restaurants held Wine Spectator Grand Awards.

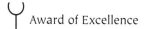 Award of Excellence    Best of Award of Excellence

 Grand Award

Fuego
Restaurant
Bar and Grill

6958 E. Tanque Verde Road
Tucson, AZ 85715
520-886-1745
www.fuegorestaurant.com

Dinner nightly 5:00pm - 9:00pm
Lunch open for private parties

 # Fuego Restaurant Bar and Grill

Alan Zeman, Chef/Co-owner
Miki Zeman, Co-owner

In January 1996, Alan and Miki Zeman opened Fuego Restaurant Bar and Grill, which has become known as a fun and lively place for a few cocktails and appetizers or an evening of superb dining. The glistening knotty pine floors and brick fireplace of the upscale restaurant are set off by the picture window views of the majestic Santa Catalina Mountains. The Rosemary Room, an intimate room that is secluded from the rest of the dining room, can accommodate up to thirty-five people for private celebrations. An outdoor patio also accommodates diners when the Tucson weather is favorable.

Chef Alan Zeman has developed an eclectic menu that showcases the New Southwestern cuisine he was instrumental in developing. Ostrich is a standard offering at the restaurant, along with steaks, pork tenderloin, duck, and poultry. Fresh seafood is also emphasized, including specialty oysters from both coasts. Dramatic flambéed dishes are a specialty of the house, and add to the lively atmosphere. Prior to opening Fuego, Chef Zeman gathered his culinary experience in restaurants, catering, private clubs, hotels, and resorts. He is also a graduate of the prestigious Culinary Institute of America, and has had numerous television appearances both nationally and locally, including the PBS series, *Great Chefs of the West*. Saturdays at 2:00pm on 1330AM, he co-hosts a radio show: *The Z'mans Restaurant Corner*, a local restaurant industry talk show that discusses food, wine, and the dining experience. Chef Zeman has also been featured in magazines such as *Bon Appetite* as well as the Culinary Institute's *Burgermeister Cookbook*. In 1992 he was inducted into the American Academy of Chefs, and was twice voted Chef of the Year by the ACF Chefs Association of Southern Arizona. Along with all these accolades, Fuego has received The Best of Tucson.com Award for Best Food and Best Service for two years in a row, and has received the *Award of Excellence* from the *Wine Spectator* for the last five years.

A special treat at Fuego is the Third-Friday Wine Event, an educational and informative wine tasting that is held once a month. Light appetizers are paired with specially selected wines.

 Award of Excellence

Fuego Restaurant

Mussels in Smoky Tomato Chipotle Cream

Ingredients

2 ounces chorizo sausage, medium
    diced
4 12-ounce portions of mussels
1 tablespoon garlic
6 ounces fish stock or clam juice

2 ounces chipotle peppers
2 ounces Smoky Tomato (recipe follows)
4 ounces heavy cream
    cilantro sprigs for garnish
4 tortillas

Preparation

IN A hot pan, add the chorizo sausage, mussels, and garlic. Sear for a few seconds, then add the fish stock or clam juice. Cover and let it simmer for 5 minutes. Uncover when the mussels begin to open, and then add the chipotle peppers and smoky tomato. Finally, add the heavy cream to finish. Serve in a bowl with sprigs of cilantro and a tortilla.

Serves 4

Wine suggestion: Gewürztraminer

For the Smoky Tomato

CUT A tomato in half and smoke it on the barbecue grill until the skin slips off. Seed and dice.

FIELD OF GREENS SALAD
with Chili Roasted Walnuts and Valencia Vinaigrette

Ingredients

1 pound mesclun
3 ounces dried cranberries
4 ounces bleu cheese, crumbled

Valencia Vinaigrette (recipe follows)
Chili Roasted Walnuts (recipe follows)

Preparation

TOSS your favorite mesclun greens with dried cranberries and crumbled bleu cheese. Toss with the Valencia Vinaigrette and then top with warm Chili Roasted Walnuts.

Serves 4

For the Valencia Vinaigrette

2 egg yolks
⅓ cup balsamic vinegar (or ¼ cup red wine vinegar), divided
½ cup vegetable oil
½ cup walnut oil, hazelnut oil, or vegetable oil
1 tablespoon dry sherry
1 tablespoon frozen orange juice concentrate, thawed

¼ cup fresh orange juice
1 tablespoon grated orange peel
1 teaspoon dried tarragon, crumbled
1 pinch cayenne pepper
¼ teaspoon ground star aniseed
salt and freshly ground pepper to taste

BLEND the egg yolks and 1 tablespoon of the vinegar in a processor. Combine the vegetable oil and nut oil in one cup. In another cup, combine the remaining vinegar, sherry, and orange juice concentrate. With the processor running, slowly pour both mixtures alternately through the feed tube. Mix until slightly thickened. Blend in the fresh orange juice, orange peel, tarragon, and cayenne. Grind the aniseed in a mortar with the pestle and then add it to the mixture. Season with salt and pepper and reserve for serving. Dressing can be made 1 day ahead, covered and refrigerated until needed.

Yield: about 1½ cups

For the Chili Roasted Walnuts

2 egg whites
1 pound walnut pieces

¼ cup ground chili pepper

HEAT oven to 350 degrees. Lightly beat the egg whites. Toss the nuts in the egg whites to coat, and then toss them in the chili pepper. Spread them on a baking sheet and bake for 10-15 minutes until lightly toasted. Reserve for serving.

ANCHO CHILI LAMB SHANK

Ingredients

2 carrots, large diced
2 onions, large diced
2 stalks celery, large diced
   butter for sautéing
6 shanks of lamb
1 bulb garlic, chopped

5 dried ancho chiles
1 pint red wine
5 quarts veal stock
   cornstarch (optional)
   salt and pepper to taste

Preparation

MAKE a mirepoix by sautéing the carrots, onions, and celery in butter. In a skillet, sear the shanks. Add the mirepoix and sauté until brown and caramelized. Add the garlic and ancho chiles and sauté. Deglaze with the wine and add the stock. Cover and simmer for 3 hours, or until fork tender. Take the shanks out and finish the sauce either by reduction or with cornstarch. Add salt and pepper to taste.

Serves 6

Wine suggestion: Red Zinfandel

Banana Burro Flambé

Ingredients

2 bananas, sliced
¼ cup unsalted butter
½ cup brown sugar
1 ounce rum
½ teaspoon cinnamon

¼ teaspoon lemon and orange zest
Cognac Crepes (recipe follows)
Strawberry Salsa (recipe follows)
fresh berries, chocolate shavings and
    powdered sugar for garnish

Preparation

IN A sauté pan, melt the butter and brown sugar to a glaze. Add bananas, sauté and then flambé with rum. Add zest and cinnamon.

TO SERVE, arrange flambéed bananas on Cognac Crepes and roll into burro, like a burrito. Top with Strawberry Salsa, and garnish with fresh berries, chocolate shavings and powdered sugar.

Serves 2

For the Cognac Crepes

2 cups all purpose flour
2 tablespoons granulated sugar
1 pinch salt
2 cups milk

4 eggs, beaten
½ cup unsalted butter, melted
¼ cup Cognac

BLEND the flour, sugar, and salt, and then add milk and eggs. Whisk in hot butter and Cognac. Let rest for 15 minutes. Ladle batter into a pre-heated and lightly oiled sauté pan to make crepes.

For the Strawberry Salsa

1 pint strawberries
2 tablespoons honey

½ lime, juice of
1 tablespoon fresh basil, chopped

CLEAN and dice strawberries, and then add honey, lime, and basil.

The Grill
at Hacienda del Sol

5601 N. Hacienda del Sol Road   Dinner Nightly 5:30pm – 10:00pm
Tucson, AZ 85718   Sunday Brunch 10:00am – 2:00pm
520-529-3500
www.haciendadelsol.com

The Grill
at Hacienda del Sol

Craig Dibbern, Executive Chef
Dan McCoog, Sommelier, Director of Wine

Voted one of the *Top 10 Romantic Inns* by American Historic Inns, Hacienda del Sol Guest Ranch Resort has quite a romantic history to tell. The Tucson landmark, built in 1929, was introduced as a nationally prestigious boarding school for girls with families such as Pillsbury, Kellogg, Westinghouse, and Vanderbilt sending their daughters to receive lessons in the social graces, college preparatory classes, and instructions on western outdoor activities. The Spanish Colonial buildings are located on thirty-four acres of desert landscape in the foothills of the Santa Catalinas. In 1948, the school was closed and the property was turned into a guest ranch resort that became a quiet retreat for Hollywood legends Spencer Tracy and Katherine Hepburn, as well as Clark Gable. Unfortunately, after this golden period, the ranch changed hands several times and fell into disrepair.

In 1995, a group of Tucson investors saved the historic property and returned the ranch to its former glory, restoring the original building and grounds. As you walk through the adobe walls to the front porch of the hacienda, the vibrant desert garden delights the senses with color and fragrance. Inside, the décor is old Tucson, with adobe walls, hand-carved dark wooden beam ceilings, and hand-painted tiles. In 1999, the restoration and renovation of the thirty rooms of the hacienda was undertaken. Restored to their understated elegance, the rooms and casitas are the perfect place to relax and rejuvenate the spirits for a weekend or a week.

The Grill was constructed in 1997, and has been winning awards for its excellent cuisine ever since opening. The elegant Spanish Colonial décor is also carried out in the restaurant, which features panoramic views of the desert and Santa Catalina Mountain. An adjoining patio and bar complete the dining area, and all are open to the public for dinner. Executive Chef Craig Dibbern has created an impressive menu including everything from wild Scottish salmon to grilled buffalo sirloin. His style is based on classic techniques with influences of the southwest such as white bean ragout and Huitlocoche Bordelaise. It's no wonder that The Grill has been awarded several gold awards from *Tucson Lifestlye* magazine, including *Most Romantic Dining* and *Best Sunday Brunch*. Sommelier and Director of Wine, Dan McCoog, is responsible for an outstanding wine list of over 1,000 wines, achieving the *Best of Award of Excellence* from the *Wine Spectator* magazine.

 Best of Award of Excellence

Dungeness Crab and Celery Root Bisque

with Artichoke Slaw and Basil Oil

This soup was photographed for the cover of a local magazine. Six years later, I met and fell in love with the woman who took the picture.

Ingredients

4 live Dungeness crabs, 1 pound each
2 tablespoons olive oil
1 cup celery, rough chopped
1 cup carrots, rough chopped
1 cup onion, rough chopped
2 cups champagne or white wine
1 cup sherry
½ cup leeks, rough chopped
8 sprigs thyme
4 bay leaves
1 tablespoon cracked black peppercorns
4 cloves garlic, crushed
4 large yellow tomatoes
6 sprigs parsley
6 sprigs cilantro

kosher salt and freshly ground black
  pepper to taste
½ cup onions, diced
½ cup celery, diced
½ cup leeks, whites only, diced
1½ pounds butter
½ pound rice flour
3 large Yukon gold potatoes, peeled and
  diced
4 large celery root bulbs, peeled and
  diced
2 cups heavy cream
Artichoke Slaw (recipe follows)
Basil Oil (recipe follows)

Preparation

COOK crabs for 3 – 4 minutes in boiling salted water. Remove from water and cool. Remove meat from the shells, reserving the body and shells. Shred the crabmeat and set it aside for the Artichoke Slaw.

IN A stockpot with the olive oil, sauté the celery, carrots, and onions until lightly caramelized. Add the crab bodies and shells, crushing the bodies with a mallet. Deglaze with champagne and sherry, and add enough water to cover. Then add leeks, thyme, bay leaves, peppercorns, garlic, yellow tomatoes, parsley, and cilantro. Bring to a slow boil, and simmer for 45 minutes. Strain the stock through a fine sieve. Place the stock into a large saucepot and reduce to approximately 1½ quarts, about 1 hour. Season to taste with kosher salt and freshly cracked black pepper. Reserve this crab stock.

IN A large saucepot on medium high heat, sauté the diced onions, celery, and leeks in the butter until translucent, about 8 – 10 minutes. Sift rice flour into the pot while stirring constantly to avoid lumps. Add the crab stock to the pot, reserving 1 cup. Add potatoes and celery root and simmer for about 30 minutes. Blend with an immersion or regular blender, then strain into another large saucepot with a fine sieve. Add the cream slowly over medium heat until thickened, about 5 minutes. If necessary, add the reserved crab stock to achieve the desired consistency.

WHILE the soup is still hot, ladle about 6 ounces into a bowl, then add 2 tablespoons of the Artichoke Slaw. Garnish around the slaw with Basil Oil and serve.

Yield: about 2 quarts

For the Artichoke Slaw

1 cup artichoke hearts, julienned	kosher salt and freshly ground pepper
1 tablespoon freshly squeezed lime juice	to taste
1 tablespoon chopped basil	reserved crab meat (see above)

COOK julienned artichoke hearts in boiling salted water for about 2 minutes until they are slightly under-done. Remove them from the water and shock them in an ice water bath. In a small mixing bowl, combine the reserved crabmeat, artichoke hearts, lime juice, and basil. Season to taste with salt and pepper and reserve for serving.

For the Basil Oil

2 cups basil, chopped	½ cup truffle oil
½ cup olive oil	

IN A small saucepot, bring 4 cups of water to a boil and blanch basil for about 15 seconds. Remove it from the boiling water and shock it in an ice bath. Drip dry the basil, then put in a blender. While blending, slowly add the olive oil and then the truffle oil. Strain through a sieve and let sit overnight.

SEARED DIVER SCALLOPS
with Oven Roasted Pineapple and Mango Salsa

Ingredients

2   U-10 Diver scallops
1   small red onion
    olive oil to coat
½   cup pineapple, small dice

salt and pepper to taste
¼   cup mango, small dice
1   pinch cilantro, chopped

Preparation

HEAT the oven to 350 degrees. Peel the foot off of each scallop, rinse scallops, and set aside. Place the whole red onion in a bowl and cover lightly with olive oil. Wrap it with aluminum foil and place it in the oven, roasting until soft.

REDUCE the oven heat to 200 degrees. Spread the diced pineapple on a Silpat mat in an even layer. Sprinkle with salt and pepper and place in the oven for 1 hour. Fine dice the roasted red onion and toss with the cooked pineapple and the mango. Add the cilantro and salt and pepper to taste.

SEASON both sides of the scallops and sear on each side until golden brown, about 3 minutes per side. Place them on a serving tray and top each scallop with a little of the pineapple mango salsa. Serve hot.

Serves 1

LAMB SHANKS

with Portobello Caramelized Onion Jus and Maytag Blue Cheese Risotto

Lamb Shanks have been very successful throughout the winter here in Tucson. With the Maytag Blue Cheese Risotto accompanied by a full-bodied Pinot Noir, good conversation, and the right company, the meal can last the entire evening.

Ingredients

4   18-22 ounce lamb fore shanks
1   cup olive oil
½   cup parsley, chopped
¼   cup fresh thyme, chopped
1   tablespoon garlic, chopped
    kosher salt and freshly ground black
      pepper to taste

Veal Stock (recipe follows)
1   quart Brown Sauce (recipe follows)
    Portobello Caramelized Onion Jus
      (recipe follows)
    Maytag Blue Cheese Risotto
      (recipe follows)

Preparation

HEAT oven to 250 degrees. Rinse the shanks under cool water and pat dry. In a small bowl combine olive oil, parsley, thyme, garlic, and pepper. Dip shanks in this marinade and lightly season with kosher salt and black pepper. In a large sauté pan, sear both sides of the shanks until they are golden brown, approximately 5 minutes on both sides. In a deep roasting pan, place the shanks side by side, and then cover with 1 quart of the Brown Sauce to completely submerge. Cover with foil and braise in the oven for about 4 hours.

TO SERVE, place 3 ounces of the Maytag Blue Cheese Risotto in a large bowl for each person. Place one shank on top of the risotto and pour 2 ounces of the Portobello Caramelized Onion Jus around the bottom. Serve with your favorite vegetables.

Serves 4

Wine suggestion: a full-bodied Pinot Noir

For the Veal Stock

3   pounds veal shank bones
      olive oil, to coat
1   cup onion, rough cut
1   cup celery, rough cut, no leaves
1   cup carrots, rough cut
6   cloves garlic

1   ham hock, smoked
1   tablespoon cracked black peppercorns
6   sprigs thyme
8   sprigs parsley
3   bay leaves
1   pint cherry tomatoes

HEAT the oven to 375 degrees. Make the veal stock at least one day in advance. Rinse veal bones under cool running water. Place them in a roasting pan and lightly coat them with olive oil. Roast in the oven for about 45 – 50 minutes until golden brown. Place veal bones in a large stockpot. Drain the fat from the roasting pan, and add onions, celery, carrots, and garlic to pan. Roast in the oven for about 15 – 20 minutes until lightly caramelized. Add these vegetables to the veal bones in the large stockpot. Cover bones and vegetables with about 1½ gallons of cold water. Add rest of ingredients. Bring to a boil, then reduce to a very low heat and simmer for 12 – 18 hours. Strain, skim fat off the top of the stock, and reserve for use.

For the Brown Sauce

½   cup onions, rough chopped
½   cup carrots, rough chopped
½   cup celery, rough chopped
2   tablespoons olive oil
¼   cup tomato paste
2   cups cabernet or burgundy wine

2   tablespoons cracked black peppercorns
2   bay leaves
4   sprigs thyme
1   tablespoon garlic, chopped
1   ham hock, smoked
2½ quarts Veal Stock

IN A large saucepot, sauté onions, carrots, and celery in olive oil for approximately 6 – 10 minutes. Add tomato paste and stir to prevent sticking to the bottom of the pan. Deglaze with the red wine, add peppercorns and reduce until almost dry. Add bay leaves, thyme sprigs, garlic, ham hock, and veal stock, and reduce by half. Reserve for use.

For the Portobello Caramelized Onion Jus

½   cup onions, julienned
¼   cup shallots, julienned
    olive oil to sauté
8   medium portobello mushrooms, with
    stems, chopped
1   tablespoon garlic, chopped

1   teaspoon cracked black peppercorns
1   cup cabernet or burgundy wine
½   quart Brown Sauce
1   sprig fresh rosemary, crushed
2   bay leaves

IN A large saucepot over medium-low heat, caramelize onions and shallots in olive oil until they are dark caramel in color. Add portobello, garlic, peppercorns, and wine to deglaze. Reduce until almost dry, then add Brown Sauce. Add rosemary and bay leaves. Simmer for about 30 – 50 minutes to desired consistency, then strain and set aside for service.

For the Maytag Blue Cheese Risotto

2   tablespoons olive oil
1   cup onion, small dice
1   tablespoon garlic, minced
2   cups Arborio rice

8   cups chicken stock
1   cup heavy cream
1   tablespoon butter
½   cup Maytag Blue Cheese

IN A large skillet, add olive oil and sauté onions. When they are translucent, about 5 minutes, add garlic. Then add rice and stir to cover with oil. Add the stock, 2 cups at a time, and let it cook down between each addition, stirring frequently. After the stock is added, add cream and butter and let it cook down. After cream has been incorporated, let it sit on low heat until ready to serve. Just before service, add the blue cheese.

TUCSON ORIGINALS DINE ORIGINALS

Tucson Originals is a local organization of independently owned and operated restaurants that provide the soul and distinctive flavors of food that help define a sense of place. They aid in the creation of unique menu items that are original to Tucson and southern Arizona and promote the use of fresh, local ingredients. Begun over eight years ago, the organization was formed to help combat the proliferation of chain restaurants which often present a bland mix of interior design and foods that fit into every place, without achieving that special sense of place.

We feature ten of the Tucson Originals in this book. You will recognize them by the Tucson Originals logo. We encourage you to try these restaurants and all of the Tucson originals. Their web page at www.tucsonoriginals.com lists all of their restaurants along with click-throughs to each of the restaurants' web sites. The site has a map showing the location of each of the restaurants and features upcoming events.

A national organization known as Dine Originals was formed about the same time and the two organizations have combined forces. Dine Originals members insist that their food is fresh, local and full of flavor. There are currently 20 chapters across North America with over 700 locally owned restaurants. Each local restaurant captures its community's flavor and unique personality.

Dine Originals has a great web site, www.dineoriginals.com, which lists all of the chapters. There is a direct link to each chapter's web site. Each chapter has a list of their members and a direct link to each member restaurant's web site. We highly recommend the Dine Originals restaurants to our readers.

Janos &
J Bar Latin Grill

Janos Hours:
Dinner Monday through Thursday
5:30pm – 9:00pm
Friday and Saturday 5:30pm – 9:30pm

J-Bar Latin Grill Hours:
Dinner Monday through Saturday
5:00pm – 9:30pm
Bar Monday through Saturday
5:00pm – Closing

Janos &
J Bar Latin Grill

Janos Wilder, Executive Chef/Owner
Rebecca Wilder, Owner
Carlos Calderon, Chef de Cuisine – Janos
Mark Babani, Executive Chef – J Bar

Janos Wilder has earned the right to be called a Tucson culinary icon. The James Beard Foundation considered him a rising star of American Cuisine, and awarded him *Best Chef in the Southwest* in 2000. He has prepared dinners at the Beard House numerous times, always to sold-out houses. His signature restaurant, Janos, has received the *Mobil 4 Star Award*, AAA's Four Diamond Award and the *Wine Spectator* magazine has bestowed the coveted *Best of Award of Excellence* on the restaurant. In 1993, he was the first Tucsonan inducted into the Scottsdale Culinary Hall of Fame. All these awards are richly deserved, but have not tempted Janos Wilder to rest on his laurels. The creativity, flavor, and passion of his dishes still stand out today as they have always done.

Janos started cooking as a teenager in a local pizza parlor in California. He continued cooking throughout high school and college and upon graduation, he decided to put his academic pursuits on hold while he pursued a career as a chef. He spent several years in the Colorado Rockies, where he began to develop his practice of using the best of what was local, starting modestly with deliveries of herbs and rhubarb, then trout from the mountain streams, foraged forest mushrooms, suckling pigs from farms on the plains, buffalo, antelope, and even rattlesnake. After the Rockies, Janos spent a season as Chef at Le Mirage in Santa Fe before heading to Bordeaux, France. There he learned first-hand the French sensitivity toward ingredients while being exposed to the techniques of classical and nouvelle cuisine.

Returning to the United States in 1982, Janos and his wife, Rebecca, located in Tucson, near her family home in Nogales. Looking for a location to set up their first restaurant, they found a unique National Historic Landmark home on the grounds of the Tucson Museum of Art. Opening on Halloween 1983, the restaurant quickly gained national and international acclaim for its inspired interpretive cooking style, blending French techniques with the ingredients Janos was getting from his growers in southern Arizona and his network of sources stretching into Mexico.

In 1998, the restaurant moved its location to a freestanding building on the grounds of The Westin La Paloma Resort and Spa, a four-star resort in the foothills of the Santa Catalina Mountains. Within a year of re-opening at the new location, Janos and Rebecca instituted a second restaurant adjoining and connected to Janos, naming it J Bar Latin Grill. The restaurant has its own entrance but is connected to the founding restaurant through common areas. The two restaurants are connected in the innovative spirit and creativity of their founder, but offer two very distinct experiences.

The soul of the Janos philosophy centers the menu around French-inspired southwestern cuisine, using produce grown by a network of gardeners throughout southern Arizona. Much of the seafood and shrimp come from the Sea of Cortez with other items flown in from around the globe. Veal, pork, lamb, beef, and game are treated with innovative preparations that emphasize the nuance and subtlety of French technique along with the dynamic flavors of chiles, corn, and herbs from the region. The global influence on the cuisine is found in the eclectic selection of menu items from Asia and the Mediterranean, as well as elsewhere. The elegant dining room features multi-level dining, in order to take advantage of the beautiful views from the large windows. The thick dark wood beams in the ceiling set a counterpoint to the crisp white linen service and complement the large comfortable chairs. A temperature-controlled storage for 12,000 bottles of wine supports a list of over 900 selections of domestic, new and old world vintages with extensive verticals in California Cabernets. Over thirty wines are available by the glass.

J Bar Latin Grill offers a very different atmosphere, but the same innovative and creative culinary view. The more casual restaurant was inspired by the Parillas of bordertown Nogales. Much of the activity centers on the bar itself, a handsome, custom-made construction of tin and mirrors, where the bartenders whip up exotic bebidas; drinks like the Mojito made famous by Ernest Hemingway years ago in Havana, and the Guadalajara Cooler, a thirst-quenching drink made of Membrillo, a Mexican quince liquor, cranberry juice, and soda. The centerpiece of the restaurant is the open kitchen where meats, fish, and poultry are grilled and served family style with a variety of accompaniments including chili rajas, frijoles de la olla, chili cilantro slaw, salsas, and hand-stretched flour tortillas. The food is a celebration of the flavors of southern Arizona, Mexico, Latin America, and the Caribbean. Dishes are prepared using ingredients of the regions as well as produce grown by local

gardeners. Along with the high-energy interior restaurant, many guests like to enjoy their dinners on the large covered porch that provides panoramic views of the entire city from a vantage point above the valley. The complete wine list from Janos is also available for the patrons of J Bar Latin Grill.

Y Award of Excellence
J Bar

YY Best of Award of Excellence
Janos

FOIE GRAS PITHIVIER
with Caramelized Pineapple and Membrillo Vinaigrette

Membrillo liquor can be purchased in Mexico. If unavailable, you can substitute quince paste and melt it down.

Ingredients

½ pound fresh Grade A Hudson Valley Foie Gras
6 ounces fresh pineapple, small dice

12 2½-inch rounds of puff pastry
1 egg yolk, beaten
Membrillo Vinaigrette (recipe follows)

Preparation

DE-VEIN the foie gras and cut into medium dice. Sauté foie gras in a very hot skillet and remove while still raw in the center. Let cool to room temperature. Reserve 2 ounces of the rendered fat from the foie gras for the vinaigrette. In another pan over medium heat, cook down the pineapple until most of the juices have evaporated and the pineapple begins to brown, caramelize, and become sticky. Let cool to room temperature.

HEAT oven to 400 degrees. Place a small spoonful of foie gras in the center of 6 of the puff pastry rounds. Place a smaller spoonful of pineapple on the foie gras. Drizzle with a little of the Membrillo Vinaigrette. Top with the remaining puff pastry rounds and crimp the edges to seal them tightly. Brush each pithivier lightly with the egg yolk. Bake for about 10 – 15 minutes until the puff pastry rises completely and browns. Serve warm and drizzle with a little of the remaining vinaigrette.

Serves 6

Wine suggestion; a nice sauterne

For the Membrillo Vinaigrette

3 ounces membrillo liquor
1 ounce fresh lime juice

1 ounce fresh shallots, finely diced
2 ounces rendered fat from the foie gras

COMBINE the membrillo and lime juice and reduce by half. Soften the shallots by sautéing them in some of the reserved foie gras fat and whisk in the lime-membrillo liquid. Let it cool but not solidify. Re-whisk as needed.

Figs with Chèvre, Dried Mango, and Port Syrup

Ingredients

1½ cups port
18 fresh Black Mission figs
 2 cups chèvre
18 strips dried mango

½ cup extra virgin olive oil, in squirt
    bottle
1 teaspoon star anise
1 teaspoon cloves

Preparation

PLACE port in a small saucepot and reduce by about ⅓. Place port syrup in a squirt bottle and reserve.

HEAT the oven to 375 degrees. Leaving the figs intact, score them into quarters through the tip and spread the quarters with your fingers. Roll the chèvre into little balls and place one ball in each fig. Wrap the figs with the mango strips and secure with a toothpick if needed. Place them on a baking pan, drizzle with extra virgin olive oil, and sprinkle with star anise and cloves. Bake for about 7 minutes, or until the cheese begins to melt.

TO SERVE, place 3 on each plate and drizzle with more extra virgin olive oil and port syrup.

Serves 6

Wine suggestion: Sangiovese, Italy

MAINE LOBSTER SALAD
with Avocado and White Soy Citrus Vinaigrette

Ingredients

1   1¼-pound Maine lobster
1   ripe Haas avocado
1   whole pink grapefruit

White Soy Citrus Vinaigrette
(recipe follows)

Preparation

POACH lobster for about 5 minutes and remove it from its shell while it is cool enough to touch, but still warm. Reserve the tentacles for garnish. Cut the tail in half lengthwise. While the lobster is still warm, toss it in the White Soy Citrus Vinaigrette.

PEEL, PIT, and thinly slice the avocado, using half for each of two salads, or just a couple slices for several amuse bouche. Cut the grapefruit supremes, sections without the membranes. Decoratively arrange the lobster meat, avocado, and grapefruit supremes. Drizzle with some White Soy Citrus Vinaigrette and garnish with the lobster tentacles.

Serves 2 as salad or several as an Amuse Bouche

For the White Soy Citrus Vinaigrette

¼   cup white soy
¼   cup pink grapefruit juice
½   teaspoon wasabi oil
½   cup extra virgin olive oil

1   teaspoon ginger, freshly grated
1   tablespoon fresh mint, chopped
1   tablespoon fresh basil, chopped

WHISK together the soy, grapefruit juice, wasabi oil, olive oil, ginger, mint, and basil. Reserve for serving.

STEAMED ASPARAGUS, MORELS, AND FIDDLEHEAD FERNS

Ingredients

1 ounce raw butter
1 tablespoon virgin olive oil
½ pound fresh morels, cleaned and sliced
   in half lengthwise
¼ pound fresh fiddlehead ferns, cleaned
½ teaspoon fresh garlic, chopped

2 ounces brandy
4 ounces heavy cream
1 pound jumbo asparagus, whittled and
   blanched in salted water
salt and pepper to taste

Preparation

MELT butter in the olive oil and sauté morels until they soften. Add fiddlehead ferns and garlic, and sauté for an additional minute. Flame it with the brandy. When the flames subside, add the cream and reduce.

TO SERVE, re-warm the asparagus and lay them on the plate decoratively. Garnish with the creamed morels and fiddlehead ferns.

Serves 4

Wine suggestion: This goes well with a light Pinot from Sonoma, or a light Côtes de Rhone

CHILI BLACKENED AHI TUNA AND WASABI CRAB SALAD

Ingredients

2 cups Santa Cruz chili powder
2 tablespoons salt
2 tablespoons oregano
16 pieces ahi tuna, cut into cylinders
    1x1x3 inches
2 ounces Wasabi Aioli in a squeeze
    bottle (recipe follows)

2 ounces sriracha sauce in a squeeze
    bottle, enough to dot 16 plates
2 ounces Bright Green Cilantro Aioli in
    a squeeze bottle (recipe follows)
    Wasabi Crab Salad (recipe follows)
2 ounces American sturgeon caviar
    chives to garnish

Preparation

MIX the chili powder, salt, and oregano for the blackening spice. Coat the ahi tuna with the blackening spice. Sear the tuna to blacken it, but leave it raw-to-rare in the center.

TO SERVE, plate the tuna and Wasabi Crab Salad with the wasabi aioli, sriracha sauce, and cilantro aioli. Garnish with the caviar and chives.

For the Wasabi Aioli

1 teaspoon wasabi paste
3 tablesoons Mayonnaise

1 teaspoon lime juice

PURÉE all ingredients and put in a squeeze bottle.

For the Bright Green Cilantro Aioli

4 ounces cilantro leaves
2 ounces fresh spinach

3 tablespoons mayonnaise

PURÉE all ingredients, put through a fine strainer and put in a squeeze bottle.

For the Wasabi Crab Salad

2 pounds Dungeness or lump crab
½ cup cilantro, minced
½ cup scallion, minced
¼ cup red bell pepper, brunoise
3 tablespoons wasabi aioli

1 tablespoon ginger juice
2 tablespoons lime juice
    salt and pepper to taste
    chives to garnish

TOSS crab with the cilantro, scallion, and red bell pepper. Thin the aioli with the ginger and lime juices. Toss the crab mixture in the thinned aioli. Drain off any excess liquid. The salad should not be runny. It will be placed in molds and liquid should not run from it onto the plate.

Serves 16 as an appetizer

Wine suggestions: an Albariño, Spain – a Verdicchio, Italy or a Sauvignon Blanc, New Zealand

Harlekin Heirloom Beets
with Duck Confit and Truffled Orange Vinaigrette

This dish is a celebration of things that grow underground. The root vegetables are drizzled with the truffle oil to accentuate their earthiness. The orange marries wonderfully with the earthy flavors, as does the rich pungency of the Parmigiano-Reggiano.

Ingredients

20 baby beets	2 ounces freshly squeezed orange juice
6 baby carrots	1 ounce truffle oil
6 baby radishes	2 ounces toasted pecans
6 ounces duck confit in large pieces	Parmigiano-Reggiano, to garnish
fleur de sel to taste	18 leaves Italian flat leaf parsley

Preparation

IF baby vegetables are unavailable, use the highest quality vegetable you can find and pare them down to a manageable size. Roast and peel the baby beets. Peel and blanch the baby carrots and baby radishes until tender.

ARRANGE the beets, carrots, and radishes decoratively on individual plates or on a large platter. Garnish with the pieces of duck confit. Sprinkle sparingly with fleur de sel. Whisk the orange juice with the truffle oil and drizzle it over the salad. Sprinkle it with pecans and a fresh grating of Parmigiano-Reggiano. Decorate with leaves of flat leaf parsley.

Serves 4

Wine suggestion: Burgundy, such as Louis St. George, that is earthy and fruity at the same time.

SALSA FRESCA

Ingredients

2 garden tomatoes, medium dice
½ red onion, fine dice
3 scallions, fine dice
2 tablespoons fresh Anaheim chiles,
    roasted, peeled, small dice
2 tablespoons fresh poblano chiles,
    roasted, peeled, small dice

2 tablespoons fresh cilantro, washed,
    large stems removed, roughly chopped
2 teaspoons fresh garlic, finely chopped
2 teaspoons balsamic vinegar
2 teaspoons red wine vinegar
3 teaspoons olive oil
    salt and freshly ground pepper to taste

Preparation

COMBINE tomatoes, onion, scallions, chiles, cilantro, garlic, balsamic vinegars, red wine vinegar, and olive oil. Adjust seasoning with salt and pepper. Refrigerate and serve within 8 hours.

Yield: 2 cups

Fresh Bay Scallop and Calamari Ceviche
with Pink Grapefruit, Mango, and Chihuacle Negro Purée

Ingredients

1   bouquet garni of leek, thyme, bay leaf,
      garlic, and parsley stems
1   pound bay scallops
1   pound deveined shrimp
1   pound calamari tentacles and tubes,
      cut to ½ inch
½   bunch cilantro leaves, chopped
½   red onion, brunoise
1   poblano chile, brunoise

1   anaheim chile, brunoise
1   red bell pepper, brunoise
1   quart assorted citrus juice
    red cabbage, chiffonade
1   small mango, diced
    pink grapefruit segments
    Chihuacle Negro Purée (recipe follows)
    cilantro leaves, to garnish
    fried tortilla arrows, to garnish

Preparation

BRING a large pot of lightly salted water to a boil and add bouquet garni. Reduce heat to a simmer and poach the seafood separately, cooking the scallops and shrimp only halfway and the calamari all the way. The citrus marinade will finish the cooking. Shock the seafood in ice water after removing from the cooking liquid. In a large bowl, combine the cooked seafood, cilantro, red onion, poblano, Anaheim, red bell pepper, and citrus juice. Marinate for 3 – 4 hours or as long as 3 days, depending on the seafood quality.

TO SERVE, fill a margarita glass half full with red cabbage chiffonade. Top with 5 ounces of the ceviche with its citrus juice, filling the glass up to an inch from the rim. Top with 1½ tablespoons of diced mango and 2 grapefruit segments on the rim. Drizzle the Chihuacle Negro Purée on top. Finish with a cilantro leaf and a fried tortilla arrow.

Yield: 2 quarts

For the Chihucle Negro Purée

2   ounces dried Chihuacle negro chiles,
      toasted, seeded, & chopped
½   cup honey

1   shallot, chopped
1   cup red wine vinegar
½   cup water

COMBINE all ingredients in a saucepot and simmer until reduced to a syrupy consistency. Purée in blender until very fine, and then strain. Adjust consistence with water.

Cilantro and Chile Marinated Salmon Gravlax
on Opal Basil and Cucumber Tossed Quinoa with Romaine Leaves and Curried Raita

Ingredients

1 cup brown sugar
½ cup kosher salt
3 tablespoons cracked black pepper
½ cup chili powder
1 side salmon, pin bones removed
1 bunch cilantro

whole romaine leaves
Opal Basil and Cucumber Tossed
   Quinoa (recipe follows)
Citrus Vinaigrette (recipe follows)
Curried Raita (recipe follows)

Preparation

COMBINE sugar, salt, pepper, and chili powder. Add the cilantro to this mixture and marinate the salmon in it for a day. Rinse salmon and wrap it tightly until ready to use.

TO SERVE, dip the romaine leaves in the Citrus Vinaigrette and place 2 on each plate, fanning out. Top the leaves with the quinoa mixture. Lay 4 slices of gravlax on each portion of quinoa, making a rosette with one of the slices. Drizzle the Curried Raita around the salad and serve.

Serves 10

Wine suggestion: Viognier, Loire Valley, France

For the Opal Basil and Cucumber Tossed Quinoa with Romaine Leaves

2 cups quinoa grain
3½ cups water
5 ounces opal basil, chiffonade
1 cucumber, seeded and diced

1 tomato, small diced
1 scallion, sliced
salt and pepper to taste

PUT the quinoa and water in a small saucepot and simmer until the quinoa is tender. Spread it on a sheet pan and cool.

JUST before serving, toss together 3 ounces of quinoa, ½ ounce of opal basil, 1 ounce of cucumber, ½ ounce tomato, ½ ounce scallions, and 1 ounce of Citrus Vinaigrette per serving. Season with salt and pepper.

For the Citrus Vinaigrette

5 ounces light olive oil
1 tablespoon fresh basil
1 tablespoon fresh cilantro leaves

1 ounce lime juice
1 ounce grapefruit juice
1 ounce orange juice

PURÉE basil and cilantro with the oil, then add the citrus juices and reserve for service.

Yield: 1 cup

For the Curried Raita

1 *pint yogurt*
1 *red pepper, diced*
1 *cucumber, peeled, seeded, and diced*

2 *tablespoons fresh mint, chopped*
curry powder to taste
salt and pepper to taste

COMBINE the yogurt, red pepper, cucumber, mint, curry powder, and salt and pepper. Refrigerate until serving.

PAPAYA, WATERMELON, AND ORANGE SOUP

Ingredients

1 *red onion, diced small*
1 *ounce ginger, minced*
1 *serrano chile, sliced*
1 *Mexican papaya, peeled, seeded & diced large*

3 *cups seedless watermelon, puréed*
3 *oranges, juiced*
3 *limes, juiced*

Preparation

IN A medium pot over medium heat, sauté onion, ginger, and chile until the onions are translucent. Add papaya and cook for 4 minutes or until slightly soft. Add watermelon purée and cook for 3 minutes, then remove from the heat. Add orange and lime juices, and purée the mixture until smooth. Chill immediately and serve cold.

Yield: 2 quarts

CALABACITAS CON QUESO

This recipe is an old friend of ours. We've been making it over the years and serving it as a side dish with many of the main courses you'll find here. If you like your food a little spicier, you can spike this up with some poblano or jalapeño peppers.

Ingredients

clarified butter or oil, to coat the pan
1 large yellow onion, diced small
2 tablespoons fresh garlic, chopped
4 medium zucchini or yellow squash, or
    2 of each, diced medium

2 ears sweet corn, kernels from
3 tomatoes, roughly chopped
2 cups cheddar cheese, grated
    salt and pepper to taste

Preparation

HEAT the oven to 350 degrees. In a large sauté pan coated with clarified butter or oil, sauté onions, garlic, and squash for about 5 minutes, until fairly soft. Fold in the corn, tomatoes, cheese, salt and pepper, and transfer to a casserole dish. Cover and bake for 30 minutes.

Serves 6 – 8

Jonathan's Cork

Fine Southwestern Dining

6320 E. Tanque Verde Road
Tucson, AZ 85715
520-296-1631
www.jonathanscork.com

Dinner Nightly from 5:00pm
Lounge open Monday through
Saturday from 3:00pm

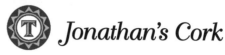 *Jonathan's Cork*

Jonathan Landeen, Owner/Chef
Colette Landeen, Owner
Peggy Forest, Pastry Chef

Jonathan's Cork has been a Tucson tradition since 1966, when it opened as the Cork and Cleaver, a chain of steak and seafood restaurants that had locations throughout the West. In 1984, it was purchased by a local businessman who renamed it The Tucson Cork and maintained its reputation as a fine steak and seafood establishment. However, when Jonathan and Colette Landeen purchased the restaurant in 1994, it really came into its own.

Award-winning Chef Jonathan Landeen, formally trained in New Orleans, brings a hint of his Cajun roots to the menu, as well as a decidedly southwestern touch to many of the dishes. Steaks still make a grand appearance on the menu as the table service comes equipped with a wood-handled steak knife when guests are seated. The restaurant serves Select Angus beef, and any steak on the menu can also be ordered blackened Cajun-style or encrusted with peppercorns. A tenderly delicious bison filet is also offered, as are a changing assortment of other wild game dishes and three fresh fish entrées nightly. Ostrich is another popular offering that always appears on the menu, and is served three different ways with several sauces. The wine list is hand-selected by Jonathan and offers a wide variety of vineyards and vintages. The list changes several times a year and offers some excellent wines by the glass as well. The Cork's well-trained waitstaff is exceptional at helping guests with selections, and Jonathan is often in the dining rooms enjoying a chance to check on his guests.

Walking through the front door of the restaurant, with its exposed brick and stucco exterior walls, guests enter into the softly lit dining areas with white adobe walls and massive dark wooden beams overhead. Two of the dining rooms offer the romantic glow of beehive fireplaces and all rooms have a comfortable ambience with western memorabilia decorating the walls and soft jazz music in the background. Tables are available on the cozy, covered brick patio year-round. This friendly restaurant is also known for cheerfully whipping up child-sized portions of its entrees, making it very family-friendly.

In addition, Jonathan's Cork offers catering services, both on and off premises for business and private parties. One other fun tradition, started in 1998, is the "Patio Pig" celebration featuring Jonathan's famous roasted pig buffets held every Thursday evening in June, from 4:00pm to 7:00pm. The lavish theme buffets feature roasted pig accompanied by the cuisine of a particular geographical area, such as Mexico or the Caribbean.

Bacon Wrapped Shrimp

with Red Chile Cream Sauce

Ingredients

16 large (size 16 – 20) shrimp, peeled
   and deveined
1 cup queso fresco, cut into 1 x ½-inch
   pieces
8 pieces smoked bacon, thin sliced and
   cut in half (jalapeño smoked bacon
   is recommended)

chopped Napa cabbage
Red Chile Cream Sauce
   (recipe follows)

Preparation

HEAT the oven to 350 degrees. Cut the large end of the shrimp so that it may sit tail pointing up. Lay a slice of bacon with a piece of cheese on top. Set the shrimp on the cheese and wrap the bacon around the shrimp. Secure it with a toothpick. Place on a baking sheet and bake for about 12 minutes.

SERVE on a bed of chopped Napa cabbage and top with the Red Chile Cream Sauce.

Serves 4

For the Red Chile Cream Sauce

⅔ cup white wine
⅓ cup shrimp stock
1 ounce New Mexico red chile purée,
   uncooked

3 ounces flour
3 ounces butter
⅓ cup whipping cream

REDUCE white wine by half. Add shrimp stock and chile purée, and bring to a boil. Blend butter and flour together and roll into marble-sized balls. Use this to tighten your sauce, and add cream. Serve warm over the bacon wrapped shrimp or any of your favorite seafood.

WARM CALAMARI SALAD

Ingredients

1 pound calamari tubes and tentacles,
    cleaned, tubes sliced into thin rings
2 teaspoons Dijon mustard, strong
½ cup red wine vinegar
2 cups olive oil
1 pinch salt
    black pepper to taste

1 tomato, peeled, seeded, & chopped
2 shallots, minced
½ teaspoon garlic, minced
2 green onions, sliced fine
1 teaspoon cilantro, chopped
    salad greens
    warm corn chips (optional)

Preparation

COOK the calamari in boiling salted water for about 1 minute, about as long as it takes for water to return to a boil. In a separate bowl, combine Dijon mustard, red wine vinegar, olive oil, salt, and pepper. Reserve this dressing.

TOSS the cooked hot calamari with the tomato, shallots, garlic, green onions, and cilantro. Add the dressing and toss again. Place the calamari on the side of the plate and dress the salad greens with the leftover dressing. Serve immediately, with warm corn chips if you desire.

Serves 6 – 8

Wine suggestion: Hanna Sauvignon Blanc, Sonoma

Rockshrimp, Cucumber, and Raspberry Vinaigrette Salad

If rock shrimp are not available, you may use 71/90 count peeled and de-veined white shrimp.

Ingredients

½ teaspoon Dijon mustard
½ lemon, juice from
¼ cup raspberry vinegar
1 cup extra virgin olive oil
1 pinch salt and pepper
1 medium red bell pepper, diced medium

1 red onion, diced medium
2 medium cucumbers, peeled, seeded, and diced large
sugar to taste
2 pounds rock shrimp, cooked & chilled
red salad Savoy leaves

Preparation

IN A medium glass bowl, mix mustard, lemon juice, and vinegar together. Blend in olive oil to a smooth consistency. Continue stirring, and add salt, pepper, bell pepper, and onion. Toss this dressing with the cucumbers and allow it to rest for an hour in the refrigerator. Check the flavor and add additional salt and pepper and a little sugar if needed. Toss in the rock shrimp.

TO SERVE, place 1 or 2 salad Savoy leaves in a large martini glass. Fill with the shrimp cucumber mix and serve.

Serves 6 – 8

Wine suggestion: Renwood 2005 Pinot Grigio

VENISON ORETTA

(Braised Venison Shanks with Black-Eyed Peas and Greens)

Ingredients

8 2½-inch slices venison shank
  salt and pepper to taste
  flour to coat
¾ cup olive oil, canola oil, or a blend
1½ cups onion, diced small
1½ cups celery, diced small
½ cup carrots, diced small

2 cups white wine
4 cups chicken stock
¼ cup garlic, minced (optional)
2 large sprigs rosemary
  Black Eyed Peas and Greens
    (recipe follows)
  Gremolata (recipe follows)

Preparation

HEAT oven to 375 degrees. Lightly salt and pepper the venison, and then dust with flour. In a large heavy bottomed pot or cast iron skillet sauté venison in the oil for 5 to 8 minutes on each side until golden brown. Remove from the pan and add onion, celery, and carrots. Sauté, quickly scraping the bottom to loosen any bits of meat and flour. Add wine and chicken stock. Bring to a simmer and gently place the browned shanks into the liquid. Add rosemary sprigs. Cover and bake in the oven for 3 hours, until the meat falls off the bone.

WITH a slotted spoon, carefully remove the venison and keep warm for serving. Strain the stock from the pan and adjust the seasoning. To serve, place venison and Black Eyed Peas and Greens on a plate. Pour the stock over the Black Eyed Peas, and sprinkle the venison with the Gremolata.

Serves 8

Wine suggestion: 2005 Two Hands Angel's Share Shiraz, Australia

For the Black-Eyed Peas and Greens

1½ cups black-eyed peas
6 cups water
1 onion, peeled
1 stalk celery
½ tablespoon salt

1 bay leaf
1 clove garlic (optional)
2 bunches collard greens
1 bunch mustard greens, chopped
2 tablespoons olive oil

IN A pot, combine the black-eyed peas, water, onion, celery, salt, bay leaf, and garlic. Bring to a boil and turn down to a quiet simmer. Cook for almost 1 hour. Do not cook too quickly. Remove bay leaf, onion, and celery when done. Sauté the collard greens and mustard greens in olive oil. Add the cooked peas and serve with the venison.

For the Gremolata

2 tablespoons parsley, finely chopped
2 shallots, minced

½ teaspoon lemon rind, grated

COMBINE the parsley, shallots, and lemon rind, and reserve for serving.

ALMOND ROCA TORTE

Ingredients

½ pound chocolate
1 cup whipping cream
1 cup plus 4 tablespoons butter
2 tablespoons corn syrup
　almond roca, in crumbs to coat

1½ cups brown sugar
2 ounces unsweetened chocolate, melted
4 eggs
　whipped cream for garnish

Preparation

BOIL the cream and combine it with the chocolate, 4 tablespoons of the butter and corn syrup. Let it stand, then mix until smooth to form a ganache.

COAT a 9-inch springform pan with almond roca crumbs. Pour in the ganache over the crumbs to form a base. Any almond roca will work for these crumbs.

MIX the remaining cup of butter with the brown sugar until smooth. Add the melted unsweetened chocolate and whip in the eggs. Pour this mousse over the ganache base.

TO SERVE, ice the torte with whipped cream and cover with chopped almond roca.

Yield: 1 10-inch round

Pastiche
Modern Eatery

Pastiche
modern eatery

3025 North Campbell Avenue
Tucson, AZ 85719
520-325-3333
www.pasticheme.com

Lunch & Dinner
Monday through Friday
11:30am – Midnight
Dinner Saturday & Sunday
4:30pm – Midnight

 # Pastiche Modern Eatery

Pat Connors, Owner/General Manager
Julie Connors, Owner
Don Kishensky, Chef

A Tucson favorite since 1998, Pastiche is centrally located, just two miles north of the University of Arizona. This upscale restaurant conveys a casual and welcoming atmosphere with its colorful contemporary style featuring the changing works of local artists. The spaciousness of the restaurant and the soft, indirect lighting, give diners a sense of breathing space and privacy.

Owner and General Manager, Pat Connors, has worked in various restaurants in Arizona for over twenty years. Thriving on the energy and passion involved in running his own restaurant, Pat also volunteers his own time and the restaurant to support numerous charitable events for the Tucson community. He was also instrumental in the founding of the Tucson Originals, promoting the independent restaurants of the area. His expertise helped in the formation of the national offspring of the Tucson Originals, Dine Originals, and he remains on its Executive Board. In 2005 Pat and his wife, Julie, opened the Pastiche Wine Shop which features an assortments of wine merchandise and over 300 wine selections as well as cookbooks, unusual gift items and baskets, and the mouthwatering desserts that are served in the restaurant.

Celebrated local Pastry Chef, Lorraine Glicksman, who received the gold award for *Best Sinful Desserts* in 2005 from *Tucson Lifestyle* magazine, creates those desserts. Chef Don Kishensky commands the Pastiche kitchen and is responsible for the creative menu and taste-filled dishes. A native of Canada, Don graduated from the Culinary School in Vancouver, British Columbia and has experienced the cuisine of over sixty different countries. As well as restaurants in Canada and the United States, he has worked in restaurants in the Caribbean and has been the chef on two private yachts. He sums up his culinary philosophy by saying, "Make your food taste good!" Ignoring the current clichés, he gets down to the basics of creating beautiful meals by using different seasonings and knowing what foods combine well, always continuing to add personal nuances to his creations.

Uniquely, Pastiche serves many of its dishes in two sizes, regular portions and smaller, bistro-style portions. Pastiche stays open until midnight every night, and these bistro-style portions are quite popular with the late-night theatre groups and other night owls. Along with the prestigious *Award of Excellence* from the *Wine Spectator*, the *Zagat National Review* has rated Pastiche as one of the top twenty restaurants in Tucson.

 Award of Excellence

Tennessee Bourbon Glaze

This glaze is wonderful on a variety of meats and seafood. We serve it with our sautéed salmon.

Ingredients

2 cups apple juice
1 cup brown sugar

½ pound butter
4 ounces bourbon whiskey

Preparation

REDUCE apple juice to 1 cup. Add brown sugar, and whisk in the butter. Then add the bourbon. Reserve for use.

Yield: 3 cups

Chile Remoulade

We like to serve this remoulade with tacos, as a sandwich spread, with French fries, and with our Margarita fries.

Ingredients

½ cup capers
¼ cup lemon juice
1 tablespoon garlic, *minced*
1 cup mayonnaise

¼ cup basil, *chopped*
¼ cup cilantro, *chopped*
2 tablespoons sambal

Preparation

PLACE all ingredients in a blender and blend. Reserve for use.

Gazpacho

Ingredients

2 small cans diced tomatoes
2 small cans tomato juice
1 cucumber, peeled, deseeded, & chopped
1 whole tomato
1 green bell pepper, deseeded & chopped
3 slices bread, no crust, diced
1 cup olive oil

½ cup red wine vinegar
1 tablespoon cumin
1 tablespoon paprika
½ tablespoon celery salt
1 tablespoon garlic, chopped
¼ bunch parsley
salt and pepper to taste

Preparation

BLEND together all the ingredients and then add the salt and pepper to taste.

Serves 4 – 6

Wine suggestion: Fuente del Conde Rosé

Black Bean Salad

Ingredients

2 cans black beans, drained
½ medium red onion, diced fine
2 stalks celery, chopped
1 tablespoon cilantro, chopped
1 pinch garlic, chopped
¼ cup lime juice

¼ cup vegetable oil
1 tablespoon cumin
½ tablespoon salt
½ tablespoon black pepper
⅛ cup sugar
1 tomato, diced small

Preparation

COMBINE all of the ingredients and toss well to combine. Chill salad until ready to serve.

Serves 6 – 8 as a side dish

Wine suggestion: Moschofilero Greek wine

Tuna Nicoise

Ingredients

1   dozen green beans, blanched
¼   red onion, julienned
1   roma tomato
1   dozen kalamata olives
1   red potato, cooked and diced
1   teaspoon capers
     vegetable oil, to sauté

1   tablespoon Dijon mustard
1   tablespoon red wine vinegar
1   tablespoon butter
1   pinch turmeric
     salt and pepper to taste
2   4-ounce tuna pieces
1   tablespoon parsley, minced

Preparation

SAUTÉ the green beans, red onion, tomato, olives, potatoes, and capers in a little oil. Add Dijon, vinegar, butter, turmeric, salt, and pepper to taste. Season the tuna with salt and pepper and sear each side for 30 seconds in a hot pan, using vegetable oil.

TO SERVE, place all the vegetables on the plate with the seared tuna in the middle, and sprinkle with parsley.

Serves 2

Wine suggestion: Benton Lane Pinot Noir

Looking west over the Plaza de Las Armas in Tucson 1883.

Red Sky
New American Cuisine & Catering

Plaza Palomino
2900 N. Swan Road
Tucson, AZ 85712
520-326-5454

Lunch & Dinner Daily
11:00am – 10:00pm
Sunday Brunch
10:00am – 1:00pm

Red Sky New American Cuisine & Catering

Steve Schultz, Chef/Owner

Formerly known as the Red Sky Café, Red Sky New American Cuisine & Catering is located in Plaza Palomino in a space that had housed a furniture store. The bright, open space is complemented with lots of windows, warm terrazzo tile floors, exposed wood ceiling beams and mellow yellow walls. Individual track lighting softly spotlights different sections of the restaurant. The black-lacquered ladder back chairs have comfortable upholstered seats, and contrast nicely with the crisp white linen table service.

Chef and owner, Steve Schultz, opened Red Sky in 1999 after holding several prestigious positions in the restaurant business. A native of Tucson, Steve started his culinary career at the age of seventeen as a waiter and then a salad cook at a French restaurant called "Roths". After five years working for the restaurant, Steve decided to pursue cooking as a career and enrolled at LaVarenne Cooking School in Paris, France. The school is named after the famous chef of the late 15th century who is reputed to be the first chef to define French cuisine. Steve received an Avance Diplome d'Etudes Culinaires from the school after one year of study.

Returning to the United States, he held positions at various restaurants in the West, including Executive Chef at the Lodge at Ventana Canyon for five years, Executive Chef at Carmel Valley Ranch in Carmel Valley, California for one year, and Head Chef at the Ventana Room at Loew's Ventana Canyon Resort for two years.

His cooking style is best described as a mélange of California, French, and Southwest styles with an emphasis on using fresh ingredients and organic products whenever possible. This enthusiasm for fresh and organic is a delight to diners, who are treated to homegrown herbs and organic produce from the University of Arizona's garden. Unique flavor combinations are a specialty, as in a beurre blanc sauce enlivened with a taste of dill, or the creamy risotto spiked with a hint of lemon. The progressive wine list is arranged according to type, starting with light bodied wines and finishing with full-bodied, heavier wines making it easier for the layperson to choose the perfect accompaniment. Red Sky has been awarded the *Award of Excellence* by *Wine Spectator* magazine.

Catering is also a large part of Red Sky's business, either at your home or office, or in the restaurant's banquet room that seats sixty-five or the outdoor patio that can seat forty. Either way, you will be treated to a menu of mouthwatering taste treats.

 Award of Excellence

PAUPIETTES OF DOVER SOLE
with Scallop Shrimp Mousse and Basil Red Pepper Cream

Ingredients

6 Dover sole filets
   salt and pepper to taste
6 dry pack sea scallops
6 peeled shrimp
½–1 cup heavy cream
1 tablespoon basil, chopped
1 tablespoon Italian parsley, chopped

1 tablespoon shallots, chopped
2 cups white wine
1 teaspoon basil
1 teaspoon Italian parsley
1 teaspoon dill
1 teaspoon chives

Preparation

HEAT the oven to 350 degrees. Carefully remove any bones from the fish. Arrange filets lengthwise and season with salt and pepper. In a food processor mix the scallops, shrimp, and cream, mixing slowly and without over mixing. Then fold in basil and parsley. Keep refrigerated or on ice until ready to use. Then carefully spoon this mousse onto the fillets and roll them up. Place them into a small pan with the shallots, white wine, and herbs, and bake in the oven covered with foil for 6 – 8 minutes. Reserve the poaching liquid for the cream sauce. Serve warm with the Basil Red Pepper Cream sauce over the paupiettes.

Serves 3

Wine suggestion: LoLonis Fumé Blanc

For the Basil Red Pepper Cream

Poaching liquid, reserved from sole
   filets
1 cup red pepper, puréed

1 cup cream
1 tablespoon basil

REDUCE the poaching liquid. Then add the red pepper purée, cream, and basil, and reduce again. Reserve for serving.

Pan Seared King Salmon

with Roasted Corn Avocado Salsa, Corn Risotto, and Dill Beurre Blanc

Ingredients

6 7-ounce salmon fillets, boneless and
    skinless
    fines herbs mix, to season
    extra virgin olive oil, to season
    salt and pepper, to season

Corn Risotto (recipe follows)
Roasted Corn Avocado Salsa
  (recipe follows)
Dill Beurre Blanc (recipe follows)

Preparation

SEASON the salmon with the fines herbs, olive oil, and salt and pepper. Sear it in a pan until it reaches desired doneness. To serve, place the salmon over the Corn Risotto and top with Roasted Corn Avocado Salsa and the Dill Beurre Blanc.

Serves 6

Wine suggestion: Voss Sauvignon Blanc, Rutherford, Napa Valley

For the Corn Risotto

1 cup onion, chopped
1 cup leek, chopped
   whole butter, to sauté
3 cups chicken broth

   white pepper to taste
2 cups Arborio or medium grain rice
½ cup Parmesan cheese
   fresh herbs to garnish

SAUTÉ onion and leek in the butter. Add the chicken broth, pepper, and rice. Simmer until al dente, and then add Parmesan and fresh herbs. Reserve for serving.

For the Roasted Corn Avocado Salsa

2 cobs of corn
1 red pepper, diced
1 yellow pepper, diced
2 tomatoes, diced
1 bunch cilantro, diced

1 jalapeño, diced
1 tablespoon lime juice
   olive oil, to taste
   salt and pepper to taste

ROAST the corn over an open flame until lightly charred. Cut the kernels off the cob. Mix the kernels with the peppers, tomato, cilantro, jalapeno, lime juice, olive oil, and salt and pepper. Reserve for serving.

For the Dill Beurre Blanc

- 1½ cups white wine
- 2 tablespoons white vinegar
- 1 tablespoon shallots, minced
- 1 cup heavy cream

- ½ pound butter
- 2 tablespoons lemon juice
- 1 tablespoon dill, diced
- white pepper and salt to taste

REDUCE white wine, vinegar, and shallots. Then add heavy cream, butter, lemon juice, dill, and salt and pepper. Reserve for serving.

ASPARAGUS BISQUE WITH LEEK AND POTATO

Ingredients

- 1 onion, diced
- 3 leeks, chopped
- 1 tablespoon garlic, chopped
- 2 tablespoons shallots, chopped
  olive oil or butter to sauté

- 6 cups rich chicken broth
- 2 potatoes, diced
  white pepper and salt to taste
- 2 bunches asparagus
- 1½ cups heavy cream

Preparation

SAUTÉ onion, leeks, garlic, and shallots in olive oil or butter. Add chicken broth, potatoes, and salt and pepper to taste. Simmer until the potatoes are tender. Discard the bottom 2 inches of the asparagus, then cut the remaining into 1-inch pieces. Add the asparagus to the soup and simmer another 5-7 minutes. Add heavy cream, blend the soup, and strain before serving.

Serves 10

Wine suggestion: 2004 La Crema Chardonnay, Sonoma Coast

Spring Rack of Lamb
with Dijon Pistachio Nut Crust in a Red Wine Sauce

Ingredients

1 16-ounce rack of New Zealand lamb	½ teaspoon rosemary, chopped
1 cup French bread crumbs	½ teaspoon thyme
1 cup ground pistachio nuts	1 tablespoon fresh garlic, chopped
olive oil to season	pepper to taste
1 tablespoon parsley, chopped	1 teaspoon Dijon mustard
1 tablespoon salt and pepper	Red Wine Sauce (recipe follows)

Preparation

HEAT the oven to 350 degrees. Trim the silver skin from the rack of lamb. Mix bread crumbs, pistachios, olive oil, parsley, and salt and pepper. Reserve this crumb mixture. Season the lamb with olive oil, rosemary, thyme, garlic, and pepper. Pan sear the rack, and then brush it with Dijon mustard. Spread the crumb mixture over it. Bake until its internal temperature has reached 125 degrees for medium-rare. To serve, slice the rack and serve with the Red Wine Sauce.

Serves 2

Wine suggestion: Cline 2003 Ancient Vines Mourvèdre, Contra Costa County

For the Red Wine Sauce

2 pounds meat scraps or bones	3 sprigs thyme
oil to sauté	1 bay leaf
1 cup celery, diced	6 cups red wine
1 cup carrots, diced	1 quart water
1 cup onions, diced	2 tablespoons tomato paste
1 tablespoon shallots, minced	10 peppercorns
1 teaspoon garlic, minced	

BROWN meat scraps and/or bones in hot oil. Add celery, carrots, onions, shallots, garlic, thyme, and bay leaf. Then add red wine, water, tomato paste, and peppercorns. Simmer for 2 hours, skimming constantly. Strain and reduce until the sauce will coat the back of a spoon, and reserve for serving.

Terra Cotta

3500 E. Sunrise Drive
Tucson, AZ 85718
520-577-8100
www.dineterracotta.com

Lunch & Dinner served daily
Sunday Brunch 10:00am to 3:00pm

 *Terra Cotta*

Donna Nordin, Co-owner/Executive Chef
Michael and Maya Luria, Co-owners

Open since 1986, Terra Cotta has become an icon in Tucson culinary society. Moving to its new location on Sunset Drive in 2001, guests enjoy the distinctly southwestern décor of the restaurant, from the rich copper of the handcrafted bar to the masterfully constructed brick pizza oven. Cool desert hues with colorful accents add a relaxed touch to the atmosphere.

Executive Chef Donna Nordin is a pioneer in the development of Southwestern Cuisine. Originally from California, Donna studied abroad in Rouen, France at the age of eighteen. This experience set in motion a compelling urge to work with food, and she soon enrolled at Le Cordon Bleu in Paris. Relocating to San Francisco, she began a teaching career that has taken her around the world. In 1976 she opened her own cooking school, La Grande Bouffe, which continued to spread her fame. She returned to France several times during the years and in 1979 studied with Gaston Lenotre, world-renowned pastry chef. Teaching appearances throughout the country led her to a three-day teaching engagement in Tucson in 1984. She fell in love with the spectacular climate and became fascinated with the unique native ingredients of the area. That year she became head chef for Tucson's Gourmet to Go, Inc. At the same time, she began to conceptualize plans for a restaurant with her soon-to-be husband, Don Luria. The restaurant was an instant success and has maintained its reputation throughout the years. Don has since passed the mantel of proprietor on to their son, Michael. Don has continued his interests in the restaurant industry as the founder of Tucson Originals, an organization started in 1998 to preserve and promote local, independently owned restaurants that provide the soul and distinctive flavors of food that help define a sense of place. Don, now President of Dine Originals, travels the country, setting up local chapters of independent restaurants with the same goal.

Terra Cotta fulfills this goal by serving "Innovative Regional Flavors", based on the fundamental ingredients native to the American Southwest and northern Mexico: chiles, corn, tomatoes, squash, and beans. It also reaches deeper into Mexico, especially the Yucatan, central Mexico, and Oaxaca, where the sauces are more robust, complex, and balanced. Using fresh ingredients and classical French contemporary cooking techniques and presentation styles, Terra Cotta creates a unique example of Southwestern cuisine.

 Award of Excellence

CHIPOTLE SHRIMP

Ingredients

  2 tablespoons olive oil
 24 jumbo shrimp, peeled and deveined
  8 ounces whole peeled tomatoes, rough
       chopped
  1 tablespoon garlic, minced

  1 bunch scallions, chopped
  2 cups white wine
  1 tablespoon chipotle purée
  ½ pound whole butter
     salt and pepper to taste

Preparation

IN A hot skillet add the olive oil, shrimp, tomatoes, garlic, and scallions, and sauté. Deglaze for 30 seconds, stirring constantly, then add the wine and deglaze again. Add the chipotle purée and reduce the liquid by half. Slowly add the butter while constantly whisking. Once the butter is incorporated, season with salt and pepper and serve.

Serves 6

Wine suggestion: Here's an opportunity to try something a little different. An Australian Grenache would be great, but you could also think about an Australian Shiraz or a Shiraz/Grenache blend.

PAN SEARED SEA SCALLOPS
with Serrano-Roasted Tomato Butter

Ingredients

12 U-10 sea scallops
   salt and pepper to taste
2 tablespoons olive oil
6 Roasted Tomatoes (recipe follows)
2 serrano chiles, sliced thin

1 tablespoon garlic, minced
½ cup chopped mixed herbs (such as
   basil, thyme, oregano, parsley)
2 cups white wine
½ pound whole butter

Preparation

SEASON the scallops with salt and pepper. In a hot skillet with the olive oil, add the scallops and caramelize them. Flip the scallops over and add the roasted tomatoes, serrano chiles, garlic, and herbs. Deglaze with the white wine and reduce it by half. Whisk in the butter until completely incorporated. Serve with rice or pasta.

Serves 6

Wine suggestion: A bright Sauvignon Blanc will really compliment this dish. However, if you want to balance and soften the spicy serrano chiles, consider a Riesling and not necessarily a bone-dry one.

For the Roasted Tomatoes

6 roma tomatoes, quartered
1 tablespoon sugar

2 tablespoons olive oil
   salt and pepper to taste

HEAT oven to 200 degrees. In a mixing bowl add the tomatoes, sugar, olive oil, and salt and pepper, and toss together. Place on a sheet pan about 1 inch apart and bake in the oven until they start to dry and char a little; about 2 hours. Reserve for use.

PAN SEARED HALIBUT
with Chipotle-Lime Butter

Ingredients

½ pound whole butter
1 tablespoon chipotle purée
4 tablespoons cilantro, chopped
2 tablespoons fresh lime juice

1 tablespoon garlic, minced
2 tablespoons olive oil
   salt and pepper to taste
6 6-ounce halibut filets

Preparation

HEAT the oven to 350 degrees. In a mixer with a paddle whip, mix together the butter, chipotle purée, cilantro, lime juice, garlic, olive oil until it all comes together. Add salt and pepper to taste. Season the halibut with salt and pepper and sear in a hot skillet for 1 minute. Flip them and sear for an additional minute. Once seared, spoon the butter mix onto each filet and place them in the oven for 3 minutes. Serve with orzo or risotto.

Serves 6

Wine suggestion: Of course you could go with a white wine such as a Sauvignon Blanc, but with the smoky flavor of the chipotle, we would recommend a Pinot Noir.

CHILE BRAISED PORK SHANKS

Ingredients

6 pork shanks
  salt and pepper to taste
2 tablespoons olive oil
2 yellow onions, chopped
10 cloves garlic, peeled
4 dried chipotles

4 dried ancho chiles
4 pasilla chiles
2 cups honey
2 cups molasses
4 quarts chicken stock

Preparation

HEAT oven to 300 degrees. Season the pork shanks with salt and pepper. In a hot braising pan add the olive oil and sear all sides of the pork until golden brown, and then remove from the pan. Sauté the onions, garlic, chipotles, ancho chiles, and pasilla chiles until the onions are translucent. Add the honey, molasses, and chicken stock. Cover the pan and place in the oven for 2 hours, or until fork tender.

Serves 6

Wine suggestion: A hearty Zinfandel. There are many great California Zinfandels, but you can't go wrong if the winery begins with an "R".

Wildflower

WILDFLOWER
NEW AMERICAN CUISINE

7037 North Oracle Road
Tucson, AZ 85704
520-219-4230
www.foxrc.com

Lunch Monday through Saturday
11:30am – 3:00pm
Dinner Nightly 5:00pm – 10:00pm

 *Wildflower*

Christopher Cristiano, Executive Chef

Sunlit by day, romantic by night, Wildflower has been a very popular dining destination since its opening in Tucson in 1998. As the original Fox Restaurant Concept, Wildflower features New American cuisine, a creative blend of ingredients indigenous to America with European and Asian influences. This inspired fare features innovative dishes with bold flavors, and changes seasonally to take advantage of the finest and freshest ingredients available. Wildflower has been the winner of numerous culinary awards, including the *Top Ten in Tucson* from the Zagat Guide and the Gold Award for *Best American* from *Tucson Lifestyle* magazine.

Wildflower's cranberry and taupe sky lit interior features suede upholstered seating and cozy curved banquettes in the spacious dining room. Its bright and cheery atmosphere during the day draws a bustling lunch crowd, and the soft lamplight makes for inspired evening dining. The ambience of the dining room is continued in the cozy lounge area. Al fresco dining is a year-round option at Wildflower. The climate-controlled and covered patio offers an intimate dining area offering spectacular mountain views and lush garden plantings.

The award winning wine list features over eighty wines by the bottle and twenty-five by the glass, offering an excellent range of options from small, boutique producers in California, Oregon, Washington, and Australia. The list is very approachable, offering something for both the experienced wine connoisseur and the novice. The well-trained waitstaff at Wildflower are happy to help with food and wine pairings. This excellent list has consistently won the *Award of Excellence* from the *Wine Spectator* magazine.

Executive Chef, Christopher Cristiano, is responsible for the creative direction of Wildflower's menu, as well as all the other restaurants in the Fox Restaurant Concepts' stable of dining establishments. A graduate of the prestigious California Culinary Academy, he perfected his skills at some of the country's top restaurants, beginning in 1993 with an internship under Michel Richard at Citrus in Los Angeles. He also worked at Spago in Chicago as roundsman for Wolfgang Puck. A native of Chicago he also worked with renowned chef Keith Luce at Spruce before turning his sights on Arizona. His energy and boundless enthusiasm for the work he loves has been rewarded with many favorable reviews and awards acknowledging the outstanding cuisine served at his restaurants. He loves the ongoing challenge of creating memorable dining experiences for his guests.

 Award of Excellence

MIXED FIELD GREENS

with Balsamic Strawberries, Goat Cheese, and Toasted Hazelnuts

This is the perfect light, summer salad.

Ingredients

1 ounce per person mixed greens
1 ounce per person fresh strawberries
½ ounce Balsamic Honey Dijon Dressing
(recipe follows)

goat cheese, crumbled, to garnish
toasted hazelnuts, to garnish

Preparation

FOR each serving, toss 1 ounce of greens, 1 ounce of fresh sliced strawberries, and ½ ounce of Balsamic Honey Dijon Dressing in a bowl and lightly mix. Stack the greens mixture onto individual plates and top with crumbled goat cheese and toasted hazelnuts.

For the Balsamic Honey Dijon Dressing

2 cups balsamic vinegar
½ cup clover honey
2 tablespoons Dijon mustard
3½ cups virgin olive oil

1 pinch ground black pepper
1 teaspoon kosher salt
1 teaspoon fresh thyme, chopped

PLACE the vinegar, mustard, and honey in a bowl and slowly blend in the olive oil. Add the fresh thyme and season with salt and pepper to taste.

Yield: About 6 cups

Warm Maine Lobster Salad

Ingredients

1 gallon water
1 cup white wine vinegar
½ cup pickling spices
1 tablespoon kosher salt
1 live Maine lobster

1 teaspoon truffle oil
salt and pepper to taste
2–3 cups mixed greens
White Truffle Dressing (recipe follows)

Preparation

FILL a large pot with 1 gallon of water, then add the vinegar, pickling spices, and salt, and bring to a boil. Add the lobster to the boiling mixture for 8 minutes. Remove the lobster and place it in an ice bath. After cooling, crack it and shell the meat.

TO SERVE, sauté the lobster chunks in the truffle oil, and season with salt and pepper to taste. Toss the mixed greens with the White Truffle Dressing to coat. Arrange the lobster chunks on top of the greens before serving.

Serves 2

For the White Truffle Dressing

4 ounces Dijon mustard
1 egg yolk
3 cups red wine vinegar
½ cup fresh lemon juice

⅔ cup truffle oil
3 cups extra virgin olive oil
1 tablespoon kosher salt
1 tablespoon fresh ground black pepper

MIX the Dijon mustard and egg yolk with the vinegar and lemon juice. Slowly add the oils until an emulsion is formed. Season with salt and pepper. Reserve for serving.

Chinese Chicken Salad

Ingredients

2 tablespoons paprika
1 tablespoon kosher salt
1 tablespoon garlic, minced
4 ounces olive oil
4 8-ounce chicken breasts
1 package wonton skins, sliced into ¼
   inch strips
   canola oil to fry

1 large head Napa cabbage, shredded
1 yellow or red bell pepper, julienned
1 medium carrot, julienned
4 ounces mizuna (Japanese greens) or
   lettuce of your choice
   Sesame Dressing (recipe follows)
2 tablespoons toasted sesame seeds

Preparation

HEAT the oven to 350 degrees. Mix together paprika, kosher salt, garlic, and olive oil. Coat the chicken breasts with this mixture and place them on a sheet tray. Bake for 15 minutes, or until the juice from the chicken is clear. Slice the breasts into thin strips.

FRY the wonton strips in a small amount of canola oil over medium high heat until they are brown and crisp. Drain, and mix with the cabbage, pepper, carrot, and greens in a large bowl.

TO SERVE, add chicken strips to the greens mixture and dress with 1 cup of the Sesame Dressing. Garnish with toasted sesame seeds.

Serves 6 – 8

For the Sesame Dressing

1 egg yolk (optional)
1 cup soy sauce
1 cup rice wine vinegar
¼ cup fresh ginger, minced
¼ cup lime juice

⅔ cup honey
1 ounce garlic, minced
1 ounce shallots, minced
3½ cups peanut oil
¼ cup toasted sesame oil

USING a food processor, blender, or wire whisk, lightly beat the egg yolk. Then beat in the soy sauce, vinegar, ginger, lime juice, honey, garlic, and shallots. Add the oils last and mix until emulsified. Set aside.

WILDFLOWER'S MARTINI MOUSSE

The cake served in this dessert at Wildflower is Chocolate Devil's Food. We chose this sponge cake recipe for home use because of its moistness and ease of preparation.

Ingredients

10 ounces high quality milk chocolate (such as Valrhona), finely chopped

4 ounces semi-sweet chocolate, finely chopped

3 eggs

4 ounces granulated sugar
    water to coat

2½ cups heavy cream, divided

¼ cup Bailey's Irish Cream
    Basic Chocolate Sponge Cake
    (recipe follows)
    fresh fruit, chocolate sticks, or
    chocolate sauce for garnish

Preparation

MELT the chocolate in a double boiler, stirring constantly. Begin whipping the eggs in a standing mixer until tripled in volume. Coat the sugar with water and cook over high heat in a saucepan until the mixture reaches 240 degrees (soft ball stage). While the eggs are whipping, drizzle the sugar mixture down the side of the mixing bowl. Keep the mixer running while you heat ½ cup of the heavy cream and the Bailey's together over high heat. Bring to a boil, remove from heat, then add to the melted chocolate and stir until blended. Add this to the egg mixture. Whip remaining heavy cream until medium peaks form, and then fold it into the egg and chocolate mixture. Refrigerate the mousse for 24 hours.

TO SERVE, pipe the mousse into martini glasses. Cut a round piece of cake to fit on top. Garnish with fresh fruit, chocolate sticks, chocolate sauce, or other item of your choice before serving. All components can be made ahead separately and assembled in minutes. The sponge cake is best served at room temperature.

Serves 6 – 8

For the Basic Chocolate Sponge Cake

12 eggs, at room temperature
14 ounces granulated sugar
2 tablespoons pure vanilla extract
10 ounces canola oil
2 ounces high quality cocoa (such as Valrhona)

½ teaspoon baking powder
½ teaspoon kosher salt
10 ounces cake flour

HEAT the oven to 350 degrees (or 315 degrees in a convection oven). Prepare two 10-inch round cake pans or ½ sheet tray pan with parchment paper sprayed with nonstick spray oil. Starting on slow speed and gradually increasing to high speed, whip the eggs, sugar, and vanilla in a standing mixer until they are tripled in volume. Sift together the cocoa, baking powder, salt, and flour, and then sift them again and set aside. When the eggs have reached the proper volume, reduce the mixer speed to medium and add the oil. When all the oil is incorporated, turn the mixer off and scrape down the sides. Add the dry ingredients, mixing until combined. Spread the mixture in the baking pans, tapping to remove any air pockets. Bake for approximately 20 minutes, or until the tester comes out clean. Let cool. Reserve for serving. The cake can be frozen, as it is easier to cut when frozen.

Chinese Chicken Salad, recipe on page 85.

Chuck wagon 1909

Kai Restaurant

Sheraton Wild Horse Pass
Resort & Spa
5594 W. Wild Horse Pass Blvd
Chandler, AZ 85226
602-225-0100
www.wildhorsepassresort.com

Dinner Tuesday through Thursday
5:30pm – 9:00pm
Friday & Saturday
5:30pm – 10:00pm

Kai Restaurant

Janos Wilder, Consulting Chef
Michael O'Dowd, Executive Chef
Jack Strong, Chef de Cuisine

The beautiful Kai Restaurant and Sheraton Wild Horse Pass Resort & Spa are a unique experience. Set on 2,400 acres in the 372,000-acre Gila River Indian Reservation, the resort offers 36 holes of golf, a luxury spa, and an equestrian center. The architecture and art of the resort are a tribute to the Pima and Maricopa people who populated the Gila River Valley hundreds of years ago. The Pima Indians trace their roots to the HuHugam (Hohokam) who farmed the valley from 300BC to 1450AD, developing an extensive irrigation system of canals, still used today, which gave birth to farming in the desert. The Pima and Maricopa tribes have always been known for their hospitality, which continues today with the Wild Horse Pass Resort.

The elegant Kai Restaurant pays homage to the tribes by incorporating many of the produce and ingredients that are in abundance on the Reservation. Kai, the Pima word for "seed," has great relevance to the community; a connection to their past, their reverence for all of nature, and the belief that the land provides them with everything they need. James Beard Award-winner, Janos Wilder, guided the concept for the restaurant. With his early involvement in the promotion of organic produce and the use of local, indigenous ingredients, he helped to design Kai's menu on the products that have historically been cultivated in the Indian community. With its ancient roots grounded in agriculture, the community has more than 35,000 acres of farms growing citrus, pistachios, olives, melons, and vegetables, and even aqua farms providing striped bass and other seafood.

Devoted to classical culinary methods, Executive Chef Michael O'Dowd passionately strives for unique plate presentations. He has an extensive working knowledge of many cuisine styles, from Catalan to Native American. His background also includes fine wines and spirits as he grew up in the vineyards while his dad was the top executive for Seagram's. His knowledge has been instrumental in winning the *Award of Excellence* for the restaurant from the *Wine Spectator* magazine. As a member of the Confederated Tribes of Siletz in Oregon, Chef de Cuisine Jack Strong brings a rare combination of Native American heritage and luxury culinary experience to Kai. He spent the two years prior to joining the Kai team as Sous Chef at The Phoenician's Windows on the Green restaurant, and prior to that he had been Co-Executive Chef at the acclaimed Eugene, Oregon restaurant, Adam's Place.

 Award of Excellence

CRAYFISH BISQUE

The green Mexican onion is a member of the leek family. Barbecue onions can be substituted. Sandalwood shavings can be purchased at specialty gourmet shops.

Ingredients

10 pounds lobster bodies
10 pounds crayfish tails
½ cup Queen Creek olive oil
2 Mexican onions, diced
2 shallots, minced
¼ cup garlic, minced
2 carrots, diced
1 bunch celery, diced
5 leeks, whites only, diced
1 cup tomato paste
2 poblano chiles, roasted, peeled, & rough chopped
15 red bell peppers, roasted, seeded, & chopped
2 russet potatoes, peeled and diced medium

1 cup brandy
3 cups good quality chardonnay
1½ gallons fish stock
2 ounces New Mexican chile dust
2 ounces guajillo powder
1 ounce sandalwood shavings
2 bunches cilantro, chopped
2 bunches pepicha herb, chopped
5 sprigs thyme, picked clean
6 cups Mexican crema
4 ounces Plugra butter
12 black peppercorns, toasted and ground
sea salt to taste
1 cup sherry

Preparation

IN A large, heavy-bottomed stockpot add olive oil and sauté crayfish and lobster bodies on high heat until they are bright red and fully blistered. Add onions, shallots, garlic, carrots, celery, leeks, tomato paste, poblano chiles, and red bell peppers. Sauté for 10 minutes or until fully caramelized. After the caramelizing is complete, deglaze with brandy and chardonnay, and reduce by half. At this point add fish stock and cook for 30-40 minutes. Remove lobster and crayfish bodies.

ADD potatoes, New Mexican chile dust, guajillo powder, sandalwood shavings, cilantro, pepicha herb, and thyme and reduce by half. Then add crema and butter. Purée the soup and add sea salt and ground pepper to taste, and finish it with the sherry. Serve in an oversized white bowl with a garnish of whole crawfish, micro celery, and cilantro oil.

Serves 15

Wine suggestion: 2001 Domaine de la Romanee Conti Richebourg, a Pinot Noir from Burgundy

SMOKED VEAL CHOP
Rubbed with Toasted Fair Trade Coffee & Piloncillo

Ingredients

2 ounces Veal Chop Coffee Rub
(recipe follows)
1 14-ounce veal chop
4 ounces Desert Succotash
(recipe follows)

1 ounce Chipotle Molasses
(recipe follows)
1 ounce veal jus
3 ounces native squash, in season,
cooked

Preparation

APPLY Coffee Rub to veal chop, reserving a little for later use. Smoke chop in a cold smoker for 20 minutes using hickory, mesquite, or cherry wood chips. Remove from smoker and lightly dust with the reserved Coffee Rub. Wood-grill the chop until the proper temperature is reached.

TO SERVE, place a nest of the Desert Succotash in the center of the plate. Cut off ¼ of the veal chop and place the larger ¾ portion on end in the succotash. Drizzle the veal jus over top. Cut the ¼ piece into 3 slices and fan them around the succotash. Place the cooked squash on the plate and drizzle it with the Chipotle Molasses. Enjoy.

Serves 1

Wine suggestion: 2001 E. Guigal Rotie Cotes Brune et Blonde, Syrah, Rhone

For the Veal Coffee Rub

1 cup fair trade coffee, ground
2 tablespoons piloncillo sugar
2 tablespoons indio-hispano chili
powder

1 tablespoon guajillo powder
1 teaspoon dried mango powder

COMBINE the ingredients and reserve for use.

Yield: enough for 3 chops

For the Desert Succotash

2 *poblano chiles, roasted, seeded, &*
  diced
1 *carrot, diced*
1 *jicama, diced*
1 *ear toasted corn kernels*
1 *tablespoon garlic, minced*
1 *tablespoon shallot, minced*
2 *red bell peppers, seeded & diced*
1 *cup nopalitos, cleaned and diced small*
1 *cup Swiss chard, washed, stemmed, &*
  julienned

14 *pieces jalapeño bacon, cooked & diced*
   small
½ *pound Christmas lima beans, cooked*
½ *pound cranberry beans, cooked*
2 *ounces veal jus*
1 *tablespoon opal basil, julienned*
1 *teaspoon Mexican thyme leaves*
1 *tablespoon plugra butter*
  sea salt and cracked black pepper to
  taste

SWEAT poblano chiles, carrot, jicama, corn, garlic, shallot, bell peppers, nopalitos, and Swiss chard in a saucepan. Add cooked bacon, cooked beans, and the veal jus. Finish with the opal basil, thyme, and butter. Season with salt and pepper to taste.

Serves 6

For the Chipotle Molasses

1 *tablespoon chipotle purée*
3 *tablespoons agave nectar*

1 *tablespoon dark molasses*
1 *teaspoon Meyer lemon juice*

COMBINE all ingredients thoroughly, and reserve for serving.

DRY AGED NEW YORK STRIP STEAK
Drizzled with Flowering Thyme Bordelaise

Ingredients

1 16-ounce aged New York strip steak
4 ounces Horseradish Mashed Potatoes
    (recipe follows)
2 ounces Garlic Béchamel
    (recipe follows)

1 bunch baby root spinach, chiffonade
    butter to sauté
    Flowering Thyme Bordelaise
    (recipe follows)
1 ounce Kai Steak Sauce (recipe follows)

Preparation

SEASON the steak and grill to the appropriate temperature. Sauté the baby spinach with a little butter and add the Garlic Béchamel to it.

TO SERVE, place the Horseradish Mashed Potatoes on the upper right hand side of the plate and put the steak on top. Slightly overlap the spinach over the steak. Drizzle the Flowering Thyme Bordelaise around the steak and serve, with the Kai Steak Sauce on the side.

Serves 1

Wine suggestion: 1994 Chateau Petrus Pomeral, Bordeaux Blend, Pomeral

For the Horseradish Mashed Potatoes

2 russet potatoes, peeled and diced
½ pound butter
1 cups Mexican crema

3 tablespoons horseradish root, grated
    sea salt and cracked black pepper

BOIL potatoes until they are soft and cooked through. Strain out the excess water. Add butter, crema, and horseradish root and whisk together. Send it through a food mill and season to taste.

Serves 2

For the Garlic Bechamel

1 tablespoon garlic, roasted and
    chopped fine
1 tablespoon shallots, roasted and
    chopped fine
2 tablespoons clarified butter
1¼ cups bacon, small diced

¾ cup all purpose flour
1 gallon half and half
1 cup Gruyere cheese, grated
1 pinch cayenne pepper
    sea salt and black pepper to taste

IN A saucepan, heat garlic, shallots, butter, and bacon until the bacon starts to crisp up. Add flour, stirring to make a roux. Slowly add the half and half, a little at a time, while vigorously whisking the roux. Once the liquid has all been added, bring it to a simmer and finish with the Gruyere, cayenne, and salt and pepper to taste.

For the Flowering Thyme Bordelaise

2 ounces cabernet wine	2 ounces demi-glace
½ shallot, minced	1 tablespoon Plugra butter
1 bunch flowering thyme	sea salt and pepper to taste

ADD wine, shallots, and thyme to saucepan along with demi-glace. Reduce by half and strain. Finish with butter and serve.

For the Kai Steak Sauce

1 plum tomato	3 ounces Worcestershire sauce
4 tablespoons black raisins	1 ounce dark molasses
1 tablespoon curry	1 tablespoon Tabasco sauce
1 tablespoon ketchup	1 tablespoon chile, diced
2 tablespoons white vinegar	1 tablespoon chili sauce
1 tablespoon tomato paste	

BURN plum tomato on an open flame and chop up. Place in blender along with rest of ingredients and blend until smooth.

Serves 3–5

Kai lobby and lounge.

Chocolate Turrone

The croquantine can be purchased at specialty food stores, or praline wafers can be substituted.

Ingredients

1 ounce praline paste
4 ounces Ibarra chocolate (Mexican)
1½ pounds Maracaibo chocolate 49%
    (Venezuelan)
8 ounce crushed croquantine

4 pounds Maracaibo chocolate 65%
32 egg yolks
2 quarts cream
Marquis (recipe follows)

Preparation

BREAK down praline paste by beating it in a mixer and/or heating it. Combine it with the two chocolates over a double boiler and melt them. Fold chocolate mixture into the croquantine and distribute evenly on a parchment covered flat sheet pan. With another sheet of parchment on the top, use a rolling pin to help flatten it evenly. Let it set up in the freezer.

NEXT, make the mousse. Melt the Maracaibo 65% chocolate in a double boiler. Let it cool, then mix in egg yolks. Blend the cream until soft peaks form and fold it into the chocolate mixture.

TAKE the base out of the freezer, turn it off the sheet pan, and cover the sheet pan with a fresh piece of parchment paper. Put the base back on the pan and spread the mousse on top of the base. Return it to the freezer to set up. When this turrone is ready, unmold it from the sheet pan onto a cutting board and store it in the refrigerator for cutting. The turrone is cut 4 inches by 1¼ inches and must be cut with a very hot knife to prevent the base from cracking.

TO FINISH, let the Marquis warm up to room temperature. Whip it in the mixer until it becomes pale. To pipe the Marquis, use the smallest plain tip and pipe four rows across the turrone.

Serves 10 - 12

Wine suggestion: 1985 Graham Vintage Port

For the Marquis

10 ounces Ibarra chocolate
20 ounces butter
9 ounces sugar

7 ounces egg yolk
6 ounces cocoa powder
17 ounces cream

MELT the Ibarra chocolate in a double boiler. Combine butter, sugar, and cocoa powder, and beat until it is light in color. Add yolks to the melted chocolate and combine. Add the chocolate mixture to the butter mixture and combine. Whip cream into soft peaks and fold the chocolate and butter mixture into it.

Bloom

bloom
NEW AMERICAN CUISINE

8877 North Scottsdale Road
Scottsdale, AZ 85253
480-922-5666
www.foxrc.com

Lunch Monday through Saturday
11:00am – 3:00pm
Dinner Monday through Thursday
5:00pm – 10:00pm
Friday & Saturday 5:00pm – 10:30pm
Sunday 5:00pm – 9:30pm

Bloom

Christopher Cristiano, Executive Chef

Like Wildflower, its sister restaurant in Tucson, Bloom serves New American Cuisine with a seasonally changing menu. It features a beautiful blend of classic American favorites with influences from European and Asian cuisines and focuses on fresh, tasty ingredients resulting in something for every palate and endless opportunities for new food and wine combinations. The well-trained waitstaff is always able to help with food and wine pairing suggestions or special requests to ensure incomparable dining experiences for their guests.

Bloom is a popular meeting spot for local business people and shoppers alike, offering a full bar, extensive wine list, and both indoor and outdoor seating. Vibrant colors and oversized photographs of bold, bright flowers welcome quests into Bloom's casually chic, contemporary dining room. There is also a beautiful glass-enclosed dining room that can seat up to twenty for private parties, winemaker dinners, and business meetings. The sleek bar features a cuvée wine keeper system, which allows guests to choose from over seventy-five wines by the glass daily. Because of is outstanding wine program, Bloom has consistently won the *Award of Excellence* from the *Wine Spectator* magazine.

Executive Chef, Christopher Cristiano, is responsible for the creative direction of Bloom's menu, as well as all the other restaurants in the Fox Restaurant Concepts' stable of dining establishments. A graduate of the prestigious California Culinary Academy, he perfected his skills at some of the country's top restaurants, beginning in 1993 with an internship under Michel Richard at Citrus in Los Angeles. He worked with other culinary legends including Jean Francois Metaigner (the legendary chef of L'Orangerie) at La Cachette in Los Angeles and then on to Spago in Chicago, where he worked as roundsman for Wolfgang Puck. In

1996, Christopher returned to his hometown of Chicago where he worked with renowned chef Keith Luce at Spruce before turning his sights on Arizona. His energy and boundless enthusiasm for the work he loves has been rewarded with many favorable reviews and awards acknowledging the outstanding cuisine served at his restaurants. He loves the ongoing challenge of creating memorable dining experiences for his guests.

 Award of Excellence

PAN ROASTED ALASKAN HALIBUT
with Double Bell Pepper Coulis

Ingredients

2 pounds fresh Alaskan halibut
¼ cup cooking oil

Double Bell Pepper Coulis
(recipe follows)

Preparation

HEAT the oven to 375 degrees. Rinse the fish and pat dry. In a sauté pan heat the oil over medium heat. Add halibut to the pan, flesh side down. Cook fish for 3 minutes, or until a golden crust starts to form. Place in the oven for 4 – 5 minutes, depending on the thickness of the fish.

TO SERVE, swirl the Double Bell Pepper Coulis on a plate, place vegetables or mashed potatoes in the center of the plate and top with the fish.

Serves 4

For the Double Bell Pepper Coulis

3 red bell peppers, chopped
3 yellow bell peppers, chopped
3 cups white wine
6 tablespoons garlic, minced

6 tablespoons shallot, minced
4 cups chicken stock
¼ cup truffle oil
kosher salt to taste

IN A large pot over medium heat, add the red and yellow peppers, white wine, garlic, and shallots and reduce liquid by half. Add the chicken stock and simmer until the peppers are soft. Remove from the heat and blend until smooth. Add the truffle oil and salt to taste.

Roast Rack of Lamb

Ingredients

3 14-ounce New Zealand Lamb Racks
   (yield 4 portions)
   salt and pepper to season

Dijon Mixture (recipe follows)
Herb Crust (recipe follows)

Preparation

HEAT the oven to 365 degrees. Lightly season the lamb on both sides with salt and pepper. Place the lamb in a sauté pan, loin side down, over medium heat and sear until golden brown. Turn the lamb over, spread the Dijon Mixture and the Herb Crust over the top, and place in the oven for about 9 minutes for medium rare.

Serves 4

For the Dijon Mixture

½ cup Dijon mustard
¼ cup water

1 teaspoon fresh thyme
1 pinch kosher salt

MIX together the mustard, water, thyme, and salt until smooth. Reserve for use.

For the Herb Crust

8 ounces day old bread
1 teaspoon dry thyme
1 teaspoon dry oregano

¼ cup olive oil
1 teaspoon kosher salt

PLACE the bread, thyme, oregano, oil, and salt in a food processor and blend it until the bread is like sand. Reserve for use.

BARS OF SIN

This dessert has been making guests swoon with delight since the day Bloom opened. The praline paste can be found in specialty baking supply stores.

Ingredients

2 pounds praline paste
1 pound high quality bittersweet
    chocolate (such as Scharffen
    Berger), chopped
¾ pound Pirouline cookies, flaked
    Chocolate Mousse Layer
        (recipe follows)

1 pound "coating" chocolate
2 ounces canola oil
    powdered cocoa
    powdered sugar

Preparation

PREPARE a baking sheet by spraying it with oil and cover the oiled surface with plastic wrap, leaving an overlapping edge on all sides. (This is to make removal easier later on). Combine praline paste and bittersweet chocolate in a double boiler and heat until melted, stirring often. Fold in the Pirouline cookie flakes. Pour mixture onto the prepared baking sheet and place it in the freezer to chill until set. Remove from freezer and spread out the Chocolate Mousse Layer onto the chilled base and return it to the freezer, preferably overnight. Defrost for 2 hours in the refrigerator before coating.

COVER the layered mixture with parchment paper and flip upside down to remove it onto a flat workspace. Using a very sharp knife that has been dipped in hot water and wiped off before each cut, cut the entire sheet in half. Return one half to the refrigerator while the remaining half is divided into bars that are approximately 4¼ inches by 1 inch. After both halves have been cut into bars, place them all into the freezer for at least 20 minutes to prepare for coating.

MELT the "coating" chocolate and blend it with the oil. The mixture should be cooled and fluid for coating. It is highly recommended that latex gloves be worn while performing this part of the procedure. Dip each bar completely into the chocolate mixture, letting the excess drip off before dipping it a second time. Place the bars on a glazing rack over a pan lined with parchment paper. Dust each bar with a mixture of equal parts cocoa and powdered sugar.

BARS can be frozen in an airtight container for up to one month.

Yield 15 bars

For the Chocolate Mousse Layer

18 ounces high quality bittersweet
  chocolate, chopped
4 ounces sugar
1 ounce water
3 eggs

1 quart extra heavy cream
¼ cup chocolate liquor (Godiva
  Capuccino, Crème de Cocoa, etc.)
½ tablespoon instant espresso coffee
  powder

MELT bittersweet chocolate in a double boiler, stirring often. Set aside. In a small saucepan, combine the sugar and water and cook until the mixture reaches the soft ball stage. Whip eggs until they are 3 times the volume, while adding the sugar mixture. Whip until cool. Bring 1 cup of the heavy cream to a boil and mix it with the melted chocolate until well blended. Fold in the egg mixture. Whip the remaining cream with the chocolate liquor until medium peaks form. Fold this into the chocolate mixture.

Michael's
at the Citadel

8700 E. Pinnacle Road
Scottsdale, AZ 85255
480-515-2575
www.michaelsrestaurant.com

Dinner Tuesday through Saturday
6:00pm – 9:00pm
Sunday Brunch 10:00am – 2:00pm
Serving Lunch during Winter
Season only

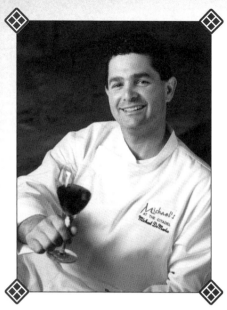

Michael's at the Citadel

Michael DeMaria, Chef/Co-owner
David Schmidt, Executive Chef

Chef Michael DeMaria is a very busy man, winning awards for his culinary skills and his restaurant, as well as hosting "On the Menu" a weekly television show on Fox 10, teaching his culinary techniques in his cooking studio at the restaurant, and running a successful catering business. Among the numerous awards, the restaurant has earned AAA's *Four Diamond Award*, Mobil's *Three Stars*, and the *Wine Spectator's Award of Excellence* every year since 2001. Michael was also inducted in to the Arizona Culinary Hall of Fame in 2002, and has participated in the James Beard Foundation's Celebrity Chef Dinner at the Royal Palms Resort. Taking his culinary apprenticeship as he says, "At the School of Hard Knocks," Michael has over thirty-two years of experience including positions at the Arizona Biltmore Resort, the Westin Hotels, the California Culinary Academy (chef/instructor), Lon's at the Hermosa Inn, and the Royal Palms Resort.

Opened in 1996, Michael's is located at the Citadel, a picturesque oasis in the lush, high Sonoran desert of North Scottsdale and specializes in contemporary Italian cuisine, using the freshest ingredients and artful presentations. The restaurant, with an indoor twenty-three foot high waterfall, offers several rooms in which to dine, all sporting a comfortable elegance, including several with fireplaces. The enclosed patios also have fireplaces; the courtyard patio, with views of a pond and lush greenery, is a favorite. Diners looking for the ultimate in culinary creativity head for the Chef's Table, a separate room set up with views of the kitchen. Adjacent to the restaurant, Michael has set up a kitchen studio, which can seat up to eighteen on comfortable ladder-back bar chairs surrounding the action. Demonstration dinners are usually held once or twice a month and spotlight cooking techniques that utilize the finest seasonal ingredients, with the final products being happily consumed by the guests. Although the evening is not set up as an educational night, often times an unstructured, impromptu class and conversation will arise, including fabulous wine discussions.

Executive Chef, David Schmidt, joined the culinary team at Michael's in 2002 as Chef de Cuisine. A native of Wisconsin, David started cooking at a local country club while he was in high school. After graduating, he decided to pursue a culinary career and selected Scottsdale Culinary Institute for his formal training, then taking several positions in and around Scottsdale before coming to Michael's.

Award of Excellence

Arugula & Endive Salad
with Apples, Walnuts, and Gorgonzola in Chianti Vinaigrette

To prevent oxidation, slice the endive and the apple just before serving.

Ingredients

4 ounces arugula
4 heads of endive, sliced on the bias
3 tablespoons Gorgonzola cheese,
   crumbled, divided
1 red apple, julienned

5 tablespoons Chianti Vinaigrette
   (recipe follows)
1 teaspoon parsley, chopped
1 teaspoon chives, chopped

Preparation

IN A stainless steel mixing bowl, lightly toss together the arugula, endive, 2 tablespoons of the Gorgonzola, and the julienned apple. Drizzle in 4 tablespoons of the Chianti Vinaigrette and toss until well coated. Divide salad among 4 individual serving plates, centering the salad. Sprinkle with the parsley and chives. Use the remaining Gorgonzola and a little more of the Chianti Vinaigrette to garnish the plates.

Serves 4

For the Chianti Vinaigrette

1 quart Chianti
¼ cup chicken stock
½ cup red wine vinegar
1 tablespoon sugar
1 tablespoon garlic, chopped
1 tablespoon shallots, chopped
1 tablespoon parsley, chopped
1 tablespoon rosemary, chopped

1 tablespoon sage, chopped
1 tablespoon chives, chopped
2 teaspoons salt
1 teaspoon black pepper
2 tablespoons Gorgonzola cheese,
   grated
1¾ cups olive oil

IN A heavy-bottomed pot, heat and reduce the Chianti to ¼ of its volume. Pour into a mixing bowl and whisk in the chicken stock and vinegar. Add the rest of the ingredients, except the olive oil. Let steep for 30 minutes. Slowly whisk in the olive oil.

Olive-Rubbed Salmon on "Cauliflower Two-Ways"

Ingredients

4 4-ounce portions salmon fillet
2 ounces olive tapenade
 freshly ground black pepper, to taste
4 teaspoons parsley, chopped
 butcher's twine, soaked in oil

2 tablespoons olive oil
1 roasted elephant garlic, cleaned
 sprigs rosemary, to garnish
 Cauliflower Two-Ways (recipe follows)
 Chive Oil (recipe follows)

Preparation

PLACE the salmon fillet on a cutting board and, from right to left, cut horizontally through the salmon, almost to the end. Fold out the top so the salmon fillet is twice as long and ½ as thick. Lightly rub some of the olive tapenade over the length of the salmon. Sprinkle some freshly ground black pepper and parsley inside the salmon. From left to right, roll the salmon like a pinwheel. It should measure 2 to 2½ inches wide. Tie the mignon using 2 pieces of butcher's twine. Repeat with remaining fillets and reserve.

HEAT oven to 425 degrees. In an ovenproof, hot sauté pan, add olive oil and salmon wheels. Sear until the edges and bottom become a nice golden brown. Turn the mignon over and place it in the oven, cooking until desired temperature is reached. Medium is recommended, when it is pink and juicy. Don't add salt; the olive tapenade provides enough.

ADD the cleaned, roasted elephant garlic and some oil to a pot and simmer until the garlic is tender and soft. Strain the oil; and skewer the garlic with a fresh rosemary sprig.

TO SERVE, place the salmon mignon on top of the vegetables in their mold. Place the coulis around the base of the vegetables. Place the rosemary and garlic skewer on top. Place a rosemary sprig into the top of the salmon. Drizzle chive oil around the coulis and serve.

Serves 4

Wine suggestion: Riesling

For the Cauliflower Two-Ways

¼ cup olive oil
1 tablespoon shallots, chopped
¼ cup garlic cloves, crushed
1 head cauliflower, whole
2 stalks rosemary
 salt and black pepper to taste

1 ounce butter
1 tablespoon carrots, brunoise
¼ cup leeks, chopped
⅓ cup chicken stock
 salt and black pepper to taste
¼ cup olive oil

HEAT oven to 375 degrees. Using a large, ovenproof, hot rondeau, add oil, shallots, garlic, and the whole cauliflower. Start caramelizing, then toss in the rosemary and season with salt and pepper. Cover the rondeau with a lid or aluminum foil and place in the oven. Cook until the cauliflower is tender in the center, approximately 35-45 minutes (check after 20 minutes). Remove from oven. Reserve shallots and garlic.

WHEN cool enough to handle, clean the cauliflower head. Using a small, sharp knife cut the flowerets into medium or small pieces. Save the trimmings for making the coulis. Reserve the flowerets, butter, and carrots for final sauté plating.

TO MAKE the cauliflower coulis, add cauliflower trimmings, reserved shallots and garlic to a blender with ¼ cup chicken stock. Blend to a smooth consistency, adding remaining chicken stock, if necessary. Add salt and pepper; drizzle in olive oil to thicken. Season to taste. You may strain it through a chinois if desired. Store in a covered container until time to serve. Note: adding oil will thicken the coulis, and adding stock will loosen it.

SAUTÉ the reserved cauliflower with butter, brunoise carrots, and leeks. Season and pack the hot and tender mixture into a round mold. Serve with plating instructions above.

For the Chive Oil

1 bunch chives	canola oil
salt to taste	

BLANCH and shock the chives and squeeze dry. Place chives in a blender, season with salt, and add a splash of oil. Turn on blender and add more oil until it is smooth and green. Stop the blending and strain the mixture through a fine strainer. Save the oil and discard the solids. Refrigerate for storage.

SHRIMP STUFFED RIGATONI
in a Chardonnay Thyme Broth

Ingredients

rigatoni noodles
olive oil to coat
2 cups shrimp
1 egg
1 teaspoon garlic, chopped
1 tablespoon chives, chopped
1 tablespoon thyme, chopped

1 tablespoon parsley, chopped
salt and pepper to taste
¼ cup cream
1 tablespoon basil, chiffonade
⅛ cup chervil
Chardonnay Thyme Broth
(recipe follows)

Preparation

BLANCH and shock rigatoni noodles and toss lightly with olive oil; reserve. In a food processor, blend shrimp for 30 seconds. Stop blending and add egg, garlic, chives, thyme, parsley, salt, and pepper and continue to blend. Slowly add cream and blend until the mixture is a smooth and pasty consistency. Using a pastry bag or zip-lock plastic bag filled with the mixture fill both ends of each rigatoni.

PLACE the stuffed rigatoni in a steamer unit for 4-5 minutes and cook until firm. To serve, stack the rigatoni, log-cabin style, in a bowl. Spoon enough Chardonnay Thyme Broth over rigatoni to make a ¼-inch layer in the bottom of the bowl. Top with the basil and chervil and serve.

Serves 4–8

Wine suggestion: a Chardonnay

For the Chardonnay Thyme Broth

⅛ cup olive oil
3 shallots, minced
2 tomatoes, concassé
1 teaspoon garlic, minced
½ cup Chardonnay

3 cups clam juice
salt and pepper to taste
1 tablespoon thyme
1 tablespoon parsley, chopped
¼ pound butter, cut into pieces

IN A heavy bottomed pot, caramelize the shallots with the olive oil. Add tomatoes and garlic and cook on medium heat for 5 minutes. Deglaze with wine and reduce to a glaze. Add clam juice and reduce by ¼ volume. Add salt, pepper, thyme, and parsley. Finish the sauce with cold butter and reserve.

SAGE ROAST PORK LOIN
on Peach & Asparagus Relish with Peach & Garlic Emulsion

Ingredients

2 pounds pork loin
¼ ounce fresh sage leaves & stalks
4 teaspoons olive oil, divided
½ teaspoon kosher salt
½ teaspoon ground black pepper

Peach & Asparagus Relish
(recipe follows)
Peach & Garlic Emulsion
(recipe follows)
micro sprouts, to garnish

Preparation

HEAT oven to 400 degrees. With butcher's twine, truss sage to pork loin and then coat with 2 teaspoons of olive oil, and the salt and pepper. In a hot pan with the remaining oil, sear the sage-wrapped loin on all sides. Roast in oven for about 15 to 30 minutes, depending on your desired doneness. Let roast rest for 5 minutes, and then remove sage.

TO SERVE, mold the Peach & Asparagus Relish in the middle of each plate. Slice pork and place slices on top of relish. Sauce with the Peach & Garlic Emulsion. Top with sprouts and serve.

Serves 4

Wine Suggestion: Pinot Noir

For the Peach & Asparagus Relish

2 tablespoons unsalted butter, diced
2 large, ripe peaches, diced
1 bunch asparagus, blanche & cut into
    coins
½ teaspoon kosher salt
½ teaspoon ground black pepper
1 teaspoon parsley, chopped

IN A hot sauté pan, add butter and then quickly add peaches and asparagus. Sauté for about 3 minutes. Season to taste and add the parsley. Reserve.

For the Peach & Garlic Emulsion

1 peach, pitted
½ cup roasted garlic in oil
¼ cup chicken stock
¼ teaspoon kosher salt
¼ teaspoon ground black pepper
¼ cup light olive oil

PUT peach, roast garlic, and ½ of the stock in a blender and blend until smooth. Stop blender and add rest of the stock, salt, and pepper. Start blender and blend in enough oil until the mixture becomes smooth and saucy. Reserve.

MINT-TIED RACK OF LAMB
on a Goat Cheese Potato Tart

Ingredients

2 lamb loins, Frenched
1 bunch fresh mint
3 tablespoons olive oil, divided
   salt and pepper to taste
   Goat Cheese Potato Tart
    (recipe follows)

1 cup yellow zucchini, diced
1 tablespoon butter
1 tablespoon parsley, chopped
   demi-glace

Preparation

HEAT oven to 375 degrees. Tie the lamb loins with mint. Rub with 2 tablespoons of the olive oil and season to taste with salt and pepper. Sear lamb in a very hot pan, then roast until desired doneness is reached.

PLACE the remaining olive oil and the butter in a hot sauté pan. Add zucchini and parsley and sauté. Season with salt and pepper.

TO SERVE, place a Goat Cheese Potato Tart in center of each plate, and place zucchini on top of tart. Cut each lamb loin in half and place 2 lamb chops over zucchini. Drizzle lamb with demi-glace.

Serves 4

Wine suggestion: Barolo

Mosaic
Restaurant

M MOSAIC

10600 E. Jomax Road
Scottsdale, AZ 85262
480-563-9600
www.mosaic-restaurant.com

Dinner Served Tuesday through
Saturday, starting at 5:30pm
Lounge opens at 4:30pm

Mosaic Restaurant

Deborah Knight, Chef/Owner
Matthew Rinn, General Manager/Wine Director

osaic Restaurant is an oasis from the everyday meal. Chef and Owner, Deborah Knight, has a passionate commitment to the culinary arts that shows in the unique and adventurous menu that is constantly updated to take advantage of the freshest seasonal ingredients. Her passion is taken up by the kitchen staff as well as the waitstaff in their commitment to provide their guests with an exceptional dining experience.

The stand-alone building is an elegant, understated structure that blends in perfectly with its Sonora Desert surroundings. From the striking entrance doors to the specially commissioned mosaic artwork on the floor, you realize that care has been taken to surround you with beauty and comfort. The synergy of gourmet food, fine wine, and a quiet, comfortable atmosphere with a professional and personable staff is the philosophy behind Deborah Knight's success. Drawing upon that concept, and her love of the arts, she decided upon the name Mosaic for her restaurant. The arts are well displayed, both in the décor of the restaurant and in the art displayed on the walls. Exceptional local artists are featured, with displays changing three or four times a year.

The dining rooms of the restaurant are purposely kept small and intimate, welcoming guests to a quiet atmosphere. The sleek, contemporary décor enhances the relaxation instead of intruding upon it. Along with the interior rooms, the restaurant offers al fresco dining on the covered patio, with its mosaic tile tables and views of the Sonora Desert and nearby Pinnacle Peak Mountain. The entire restaurant is smoke-free, including the dining patio and the covered patio adjoining the lounge.

Wine Director, Matt Rinn, has selected over four hundred different bottlings, including multiple vintages from several wineries. They are carefully chosen to satisfy the wine connoisseur as well as the novice. The wine storage has been incorporated into the building's design with a stunning wall of glass-encased and temperature-controlled wine visible from the foyer. The *Wine Spectator* has awarded the restaurant the *Award of Excellence* since 2002.

Chef Knight's culinary expertise is evident in the unique combinations on the menu. In fact, it can be very difficult to settle on only one or two dishes from the innovative menu. For those who can't decide, the restaurant offers three different five-course tasting menus nightly, allowing the diner to enjoy smaller plates of items on that evening's menu. The diner can choose from three difference themes: Vegetarian, Ocean, and Mosaic; and wine pairings are also available for these tasting menus.

 Award of Excellence

RED ORACH AND SPINACH SALAD
with Mandarin-Curry Dressing

Red orach is a great leafy vegetable that is a little unusual.

Ingredients

2 cups red orach
2 cups spinach
1 cup mizuna
1 medium red heirloom tomato,
    julienned
1 medium yellow heirloom tomato,
    julienned

3 mandarin oranges, cut in supremes
½ cup Spanish almonds, toasted
    salt and white pepper to taste
    Mandarin-Curry Dressing
    (recipe follows)

Preparation

COMBINE lettuces, tomatoes, mandarin oranges and almonds. Add dressing to taste, toss, and serve.

Serves 4

Wine suggestion: Mont Moscal-brut Cava, Spain

For the Mandarin-Curry Dressing

2 tablespoons mandarin juice
1 cup yogurt
½ cup crème fraîche
2 tablespoons apple cider vinegar
1 splash seasoned rice wine vinegar

3 tablespoons manuka honey
¾ tablespoon curry powder
1½ teaspoons orange spice tea, finely
    ground
    salt and white pepper to taste

COMBINE all ingredients in a bowl. Whisk to combine and adjust seasoning with salt and pepper.

SEARED AHI TUNA AND YELLOW TOMATO
Broiled with Turmeric Spiced Butter and Berbere Sauce

This is a personal favorite of the chef. The recipes for the Turmeric Spiced Butter and the dry spice mix used in the Berbere Sauce make more than is needed for the four servings, but they can be stored in the refrigerator or spice cabinet, respectively, for future use.

Ingredients

½ pound unsalted high quality butter, like Plugra
2 whole green cardamom
1 teaspoon turmeric
½ Spanish onion, small dice
2 garlic cloves, slice
1½ inches ginger, thinly slice
1 cinnamon stick
2 cloves
½ teaspoon nutmeg, freshly grated
½ lemon, juice of
4 yellow heirloom tomato, sliced into 4 slices each

salt and pepper to taste
fresh herbs (parsley, chive, oregano, thyme), chopped & to taste
4 3-ounce ahi tuna portions, sushi grade
salt and Madagascar black pepper to taste
3 teaspoons canola oil
Berbere Sauce (recipe follows)
micro cilantro or chives for garnish

Preparation

TO MAKE the Turmeric Spiced Butter, melt butter on low heat and add cardamom, turmeric, onion, garlic, ginger, cinnamon stick, cloves, nutmeg, and lemon juice. Infuse over low heat for 10 minutes and off the heat for another 10 minutes. Strain, and hold aside.

HEAT broiler and place tomatoes on baking sheet. Season with salt, pepper, herbs and a heavy drizzle of the Turmeric Spiced Butter. Broil until hot, but soft. Do not overcook.

Season tuna pieces with salt and Madagascar pepper and sear on all sides in hot pan with canola oil, to rare. Slice tuna.

TO SERVE, place 1 broiled tomato on each plate, and drizzle with a little Turmeric Spiced Butter. Fan the sliced tuna to 1 side of tomato. Garnish with dots of the spice Berbere Sauce and micro cilantro or chives.

Serves 4 as an appetizer

Wine suggestion: Clerico, dolcetto, "Visadi", Piedmont, Italy

For the Berbere Sauce

2 red bell peppers
2 teaspoons Berbere Dry Spice Mix, or
 to taste (recipe follows)

1 teaspoon mint honey, or to taste
salt to taste

OVER a grill or gas burner, char bell peppers. Place in a bowl and cover with plastic wrap. Cool to warm in refrigerator. Remove pepper and peel and seed them. Purée well in a blender with a splash of water. Season with Berbere Dry Spice Mix, honey, and salt. Adjust seasonings to the heat level you want.

For the Berbere Dry Spice Mix

¾ cup cayenne
¼ cup paprika
2 tablespoons kosher salt
1 tablespoon ground black pepper
¼ tablespoon dried mint
¼ teaspoon ground allspice
1 teaspoon ground cumin
½ teaspoon ground coriander

1 teaspoon ground ginger
½ teaspoon ground cardamom
½ teaspoon ground fenugreek
1 teaspoon ground nutmeg
½ teaspoon ground cinnamon
½ teaspoon ground clove
½ teaspoon onion powder

COMBINE all ingredients in a bowl and whisk together. Store unused portion in an airtight container in a dark space.

CASHEW CRUSTED MONKFISH
with Channa Dal-Carrot Curry Sauce and Black Mustard & Cumin Spiced Ratatouille

Ingredients

¼ cup rice flour
¾ cup cashews
1 pinch salt
1 pinch white pepper
¼ teaspoon ground cumin
¼ teaspoon hot Hungarian paprika
4 7-ounce monkfish portions
  salt & white pepper to taste
3 teaspoons fresh herbs (parsley, thyme, chives), chopped

4 tablespoons canola or soy oil
  Channa Dal-Carrot Curry Sauce
   (recipe follows)
  Ratatouille (recipe follows)
½ teaspoon seasoned rice vinegar
1 pinch salt
1 drop orange juice
4 ounces micro fenugreek greens

Preparation

GRIND cashews and rice flour in spice grinder until fine, but be careful not to grind too much, as the cashews will turn into cashew butter. Add salt, pepper, cumin, and paprika and combine.

HEAT oven to 400 degrees. Lightly season fish with salt, pepper, and herbs. Dust well with the cashew crust, pressing to set. Heat a sauté pan and add oil. Sear monkfish on top side until golden. Turn over and place pan in oven to finish to preferred doneness, about 6 minutes for medium rare.

WHILE monkfish is finishing, combine rice vinegar, salt, and orange juice and toss micro greens with this mixture.

TO PLATE, in wide, deep bowls or 12-inch plates, spoon the Channa Dal-Carrot Curry Sauce in the center. Mold a round of Ratatouille in the center of that. Place monkfish on Ratatouille, and garnish with micro greens.

Serves 4

Wine suggestion: Tablas Creek "Cote de Tablas Blanc", Paso Robles. A blend of viognier, marsanne, grenache blanc, and roussane.

For the Channa Dal-Carrot Curry Sauce

Channa dal is a lentil with a sweet, nutty flavor. It is very popular in India.

1 teaspoon canola oil	1 teaspoon ground coriander
1 teaspoon shallot, minced	1 cup channa dal, cooked
2 inches ginger, finely minced	1 teaspoon cornstarch
1 ounce white wine	⅛ cup water
16 carrots, juice of	1 teaspoon soy sauce
3 teaspoons black mustard seed, roasted	salt & white pepper to taste
1½ teaspoons ground cardamom	

HEAT a saucepan until very hot, add oil, and sauté shallots and ginger. Deglaze with wine, reduce au sec, and add carrot juice, then mustard seeds, cardamom, and coriander. Simmer 10 minutes and add cooked channa dal. Make a slurry with cornstarch and water and whisk in a small amount at a time, until slightly thickened. Make sure the sauce returns to a boil after each addition of slurry until nape. Add soy sauce and adjust seasonings with salt and pepper. Hold aside hot.

For the Ratatouille

¾ teaspoon cumin seeds	1½ teaspoons ginger, minced
1 teaspoon black mustard seeds	¼ cup red bell pepper, small dice
½ cup Japanese eggplant, small dice	¼ cup yellow bell pepper, small dice
½ cup zucchini, small dice	2 ounces white wine
1 teaspoon salt	1 teaspoon turmeric
2 teaspoons canola oil	¼ teaspoon ground fenugreek
½ cup red onion, small dice	½ teaspoon sugar
½ cup chayote, small dice	1 teaspoon seasoned rice vinegar
1½ teaspoons garlic, minced	salt and white pepper to taste

HEAT oven to 350 degrees. Place cumin and mustard seeds on a pan and toast in oven until the essential oils become aromatic, about 4 minutes. Cool and grind in a spice grinder and set aside. In a bowl, toss zucchini and eggplant with salt. Drain in a fine mesh strainer for 10 minutes. Damp dry in a kitchen towel, removing excess salt. Heat a large sauté pan until very hot. Add canola oil and sauté eggplant, zucchini, red onion, and chayote. Add garlic, ginger, and bell peppers and sauté. Deglaze with white wine and then add turmeric, fenugreek, and toasted cumin and mustard seeds, tossing well. Add sugar and vinegar; toss well and reduce excess liquid. Adjust seasonings with salt and pepper.

Madagascar Pepper Dusted Venison Loin

with Vanilla Risotto and Black Mountain Huckleberry Sauce

This is a customer favorite at Mosaic.

Ingredients

4 7-ounce venison loin portions
1 heavy sprinkle Madagascar black
 peppercorns, roughly ground
 kosher salt to taste
 fresh herbs, chopped
1 tablespoon canola oil

Vanilla Risotto (recipe follows)
Black Mountain Huckleberry Sauce
 (recipe follows)
Sautéed Vegetables (recipe follows)
fresh thyme and oregano, to garnish

Preparation

HEAT oven to 500 degrees. Season venison with salt, fresh herbs, and pepper. Heat a sauté pan and add canola oil. Sear venison on all sides and transfer to a baking pan. Finish in oven until desired doneness; about 8 minutes for medium rare.

TO SERVE, place a scoopful of Vanilla Risotto in the center of each plate. Ladle Black Mountain Huckleberry Sauce around. Cut venison loins in half, on the bias, and arrange on the risotto, to the left of center. Place Sautéed Vegetables in a decorative manner on the risotto, to the right of center. Garnish with fresh thyme and oregano.

Serves 4

Wine suggestion: Shiraz, Penfold's, South Australia

For the Vanilla Risotto

8 cups unsalted chicken stock
2 vanilla bean, split & scraped, divided
1 teaspoon Madagascar vanilla extract
 kosher salt & white pepper to taste

1 tablespoon canola oil
2 tablespoons shallots, minced
2 cups Carnaroli rice
1 cup heavy cream

IN A saucepot, place chicken stock, 1 of the vanilla beans, and vanilla extract. Warm the mixture and infuse for 20 minutes, then keep hot. In another pot, heat canola oil and add shallots. Reduce heat and sauté until translucent. Add rice and toast slightly. By ladlefuls, add vanilla-scented stock, stirring in slowly. Keep adding stock by the ladleful and continue stirring, as the stock is absorbed into the rice. Taste often to check doneness. Rice should be creamy in texture, yet al dente. It should take about 20 minutes, and about 5-6 cups of stock. While cooking risotto, infuse cream with the other vanilla bean. When risotto is done, add ladles of the vanilla cream, until it has reached the right consistency. It should be about 2-3 ladles full. Adjust seasoning with salt and white pepper.

For the Black Mountain Huckleberry Sauce

- 2 cups huckleberries
- ⅓ cup sugar
- 2 cups ruby port
- 4 sprigs thyme
- 1 sprig oregano

- 8 black peppercorns
- 2 cups demi-glace
  - salt and white pepper to taste
- 1 dash cabernet vinegar

PLACE huckleberries, sugar, and port in a saucepot. Place thyme, oregano, and black peppercorns in a sachet of cheesecloth. Place in pot and bring to a simmer. Reduce liquid by ¾ and add demi-glace. Cool, and remove sachet. Purée in a blender. Return to stove and heat. Allow to reduce to nape, if necessary. Adjust seasonings with salt and white pepper, and add a dash of cabernet vinegar to balance acids.

For Sautéed Vegetables

- 4 petite purple dragon carrots
- 2 bunches asparagus
- 8 yellow patty pans

- 4 baby zucchini
  - salt, white pepper, and herbs to taste
- 2 teaspoons canola oil

PREPARE an ice bath in a bowl. Bring a pot of water to boil. Cook each set of vegetables separately to desired doneness; al dente is suggested. As they become done, place in ice bath to cool. All vegetables may be placed together. In a sauté pan, heat canola oil. Add cooked vegetables with a little water to create steam, and cook until heated through. Season with salt, pepper, and herbs.

MEXICAN OREGANO DUSTED ANTELOPE LOIN

with Creamy Farro and Australian Bush Tomato Sauce

According to the igourmet website, Australian bush tomatoes are actually berries. Dark brown, with a fruity caramel-like flavor and a tangy acidity, they taste somewhat like green tomatoes.

Ingredients

6 3-ounce portions antelope loin
   kosher salt & black pepper to taste
   freshly chopped herb mix (parsley,
      chive, thyme, oregano) to taste
   ground Mexican oregano to taste

   Australian Bush Tomato Sauce
      (recipe follows)
   Creamy Farro (recipe follows)
   Chocolate mint sprigs, to garnish

Preparation

HEAT oven to 400 degrees and heat grill. Season antelope loins with salt, pepper, and herbs. Mark on the hot grill and finish in oven for 4 minutes, or until medium rare. Let rest, and slice diagonally in half.

TO SERVE, place a ladleful of Australian Bush Tomato Sauce in the center of a white round plate. Place a dollop of Creamy Farro in the center of the sauce. Place antelope loin upon the farro and garnish with sprigs of chocolate mint.

Serves 6 as an appetizer

Wine suggestion: Alvaro Palacios, carinena, grenacha, "Les Terrasses", Priorat, Spain

For the Australian Bush Tomato Sauce

2 teaspoons canola oil
5 Spanish onions, chopped
2 garlic cloves, rough chopped
1 cup sun-dried tomatoes
1 cup dry white wine
3 stems fresh thyme
1 stem fresh oregano
2 stems chocolate mint

4 stems spearmint
1 tablespoon tamarind concentrate
1 tablespoon bittersweet chocolate
1 teaspoon instant espresso
3 cups demi-glace
4 tablespoons Australian bush tomatoes
   salt & white pepper to taste

SAUTÉ onions in canola oil. Add garlic and sauté. Add sun-dried tomatoes and deglaze with wine. Reduce au sec. Add all herbs, chocolate espresso, and demi-glace, and then add bush tomatoes, combine, and simmer for 20 minutes. Purée in a blender and strain through a fine chinois. Adjust seasoning with salt and pepper. This sauce can be made before and warmed as needed.

For the Creamy Farro

2 cups cooked farro
2 teaspoons canola oil
1 teaspoon garlic, minced
1 teaspoon shallot, minced

⅓ cup heavy cream
⅓ cup mascarpone
   kosher salt and white pepper to taste
2 teaspoons freshly chopped herb mix

ADD canola oil to a hot sauté pan. Turn down heat and add garlic and shallot. Sauté until translucent. Add cooked farro and cream. Reduce slightly and add mascarpone. Add chopped herbs and season with salt and pepper.

Phoenix courthouse and plaza 1896

North

NoRTH

modern italian cuisine

15024 N. Scottsdale Road #160
Scottsdale, AZ 85254
480-948-2055
www.foxcr.com

Lunch Monday through Saturday
11:00am – 3:00pm
Sunday Brunch Noon – 3:00pm
Dinner Sunday through Thursday
4:00pm – 9:30pm
Friday & Saturday 4:00pm – 10:00pm

North

Christopher Cristiano, Executive Chef

Taking its cue from an Italian trattoria, North offers a contemporary approach to modern Italian cuisine. Its upbeat, urban ambiance has made it one of the most popular places to wine and dine. At North, where rustic cuisine and urban elegance come together, your senses are greeted by the delicious aroma of fresh brick oven baked pizzas, the bright flavors of fresh vegetables and herbs, seasonally inspired hot and cold antipasti, unique pasta dishes, and many oven roasted dishes. The wine list offers a wonderful selection of boutique Italian selections from small, regional wineries with most being available by the glass, terzo (third of a bottle), and by the bottle.

Like a cosmopolitan loft, the interior sports upholstered white leather booths, dark-stained wood floors, brick accent walls, and an open kitchen where guests can view the action as the highly skilled kitchen staff prepares their food. The floor to ceiling windows overlook alfresco dining areas with granite topped tables for dining and oversized teak lounge furniture for relaxing. North's menu, wine list, and outstanding friendly service provide all the ingredients for an unforgettable dining experience.

Executive Chef, Christopher Cristiano, is responsible for the creative direction of North's menu, as well as all the other restaurants in the Fox Restaurant Concepts' stable of dining establishments. A graduate of the prestigious California Culinary Academy, he perfected his skills at some of the country's top restaurants, beginning in 1993 with an internship under Michel Richard at Citrus in Los Angeles. He worked with other culinary legends including Jean Francois Metaigner (the legendary chef of L'Orangerie) at La Cachette in Los Angeles and then on to Spago in Chicago, where he worked as roundsman for Wolfgang Puck. In 1996, Christopher returned to his hometown of Chicago where he worked with renowned chef Keith Luce at Spruce before turning his sights on Arizona. His energy and boundless enthusiasm for the work he loves has been rewarded with many favorable reviews and awards acknowledging the outstanding cuisine served at his restaurants. He loves the ongoing challenge of creating memorable dining experiences for his guests.

Tuscan Bread Salad

Ingredients

4 slices Italian bread, 1 inch thick
4 ounces mixed greens
6 ounces fresh mozzarella, cut into bite-size pieces
2 large vine-ripened tomatoes, medium dice

1 small red onion, minced
½ cup extra virgin Italian olive oil
¼ cup balsamic vinegar
1 teaspoon salt
¼ teaspoon ground pepper

Preparation

PLACE bread on a pre-heated grill and cook until it is golden brown. Pull bread apart into medium-sized pieces. Place the mixed greens, mozzarella, tomatoes, and onions in a bowl and add the bread. Lightly toss together. Add olive oil, balsamic vinegar, and salt and pepper, tossing it all together until the ingredients are coated.

Serves 4

Asparagus Risotto

This recipe is a perfect accompaniment to any meal, or with the addition of a protein, it makes an excellent meal in itself.

Ingredients

6 ounces butter, divided
½ medium onion, small dice
1 pound Arborio rice
2 cups white wine

4 cups vegetable stock or water
1 bunch green or white asparagus, medium dice
1 cup grated Parmesan cheese

Preparation

PLACE 2 ounces of the butter in a large pot and lightly sauté onion until translucent. Add rice and stir for a few minutes, then pour the wine into the mixture. Reduce by half and slowly start adding the stock, stirring constantly, until the rice is al dente. At this point, add the diced asparagus and continue to cook until the rice texture is to your liking. When the risotto is cooked, finish by adding the rest of the butter and Parmesan for a creamy rich texture.

Serves 6 - 8

BOWTIE PASTA
with Grilled Chicken Breasts and Oven-Roasted Roma Tomatoes

The spinach and tomatoes in this dish add to its richness of flavor and color.

Ingredients

4 chicken breasts
2 teaspoons fresh thyme, chopped
2 teaspoons fresh oregano, chopped
1 tablespoon whole grain mustard
4 ounces olive oil
2 teaspoons fresh garlic, chopped
1 cup pine nuts
2 pounds bowtie pasta
8 ounces fresh spinach

4 tablespoons unsalted butter
   Oven-Roasted Roma Tomatoes
   (recipe follows)
2 tablespoons Parmesan cheese, grated
2 tablespoons fresh parsley, chopped,
   divided
   fresh Parmesan cheese, shaved
   extra virgin olive oil, as desired

Preparation

PLACE the chicken breasts in a shallow dish. Mix thyme, oregano, mustard, olive oil, and garlic together and add to the chicken. Cover and marinate in the refrigerator for at least 2 hours.

HEAT oven to 325 degrees. Place the pine nuts on a sheet tray and spread evenly. Put in the same oven as the tomatoes for 20 minutes, or until golden brown. Set aside.

REMOVE chicken from the marinade and lightly salt and pepper each piece. Cook on a pre-heated grill for about 5 minutes on each side, or until the juices run clear. Slice in 2-inch sections and set aside. Cook the bowtie pasta in a large pot of salted boiling water, drain well, and set aside.

SAUTÉ spinach in the butter. When spinach begins to wilt, add the Oven-Roasted Roma Tomatoes and cook together for 5 minutes. Add the pasta and pine nuts to the mixture along with the grated Parmesan cheese and 1 tablespoon of the parsley. Season with salt and pepper to taste. Place the mixture in a serving bowl, and top with the sliced grilled chicken breast. Garnish with shaved Parmesan, the remaining parsley, and drizzle with olive oil as desired.

For the Roasted Roma Tomatoes

1 pound roma tomatoes
4 teaspoons fresh thyme, chopped
3 teaspoons salt

½ teaspoon ground black pepper
4 ounces olive oil

HEAT the oven to 325 degrees. Core and quarter the tomatoes. Place them in a bowl and add thyme, salt, pepper, and olive oil. Toss until lightly coated. Place the tomatoes on a baking sheet and cook in the oven for 1½ hours, or until soft. Set aside.

Serves 4

CHICKEN LASAGNA

A wonderful contemporary take on an old classic. This dish has been on the menu at North since the day it opened and remains one of the most requested dishes.

Ingredients

2 ounces extra virgin olive oil, divided
4 ounces spinach, blanched
4 ounces mixed mushrooms (such as shiitake, crimini, oyster)
12 ounces pulled chicken
1 ounce garlic, minced
6 ounces vegetable stock
3 ounces butter

1 teaspoon kosher salt
fresh ground black pepper
4 ounces medium tomatoes, diced
1 ounce white wine
1 package lasagna noodles (or fresh pasta)
white truffle oil to garnish
fresh tarragon sprigs to garnish

Preparation

HEAT 1 ounce of the olive oil in a sauté pan over medium heat. Sauté the spinach and mushrooms. Once the mushrooms become golden, add the chicken and garlic, and lightly sauté. Add the stock, reserving a small amount for later use, and reduce by half. Add the butter and stir until the butter richens the mixture. Add the salt and pepper to taste and set aside.

HEAT a sauté pan; add 1 ounce of olive oil, the tomatoes, and white wine. Cook until the tomatoes are soft and reserve. Cook the lasagna noodles according to the package directions.

ASSEMBLE individual servings on 4 plates. Begin with a layer of lasagna, followed by a layer of the chicken mixture, another pasta layer, and a final layer of the tomato mixture. Drizzle with the truffle oil and tarragon and a small amount of the reserved vegetable stock. Serve immediately.

Serves 4

The Scottsdale Post Office and Grocery circa 1899.

Razz's Restaurant

Razz's

10315 North Scottsdale Road
Scottsdale, AZ 85253
480-905-1308
www.razzsrestaurant.com

Serving Dinner Tuesday through
Saturday starting at 5:00pm

Razz's Restaurant

Razz Kamnitzer, Chef/Co-Owner
Bobbi Jo Haynes, Co-Owner

Chef Erasmo "Razz" Kamnitzer, along with his wife Bobbi Jo Haynes, opened Razz's Restaurant and Bar in 1995 and immediately started receiving excellent reviews. In 1996, *Esquire* magazine's food critic named it as one the *25 Best New Restaurants in the USA* and the following year, the New Times food critic dubbed it, "The best place to entertain foodies." The Chef's Association of Greater Phoenix named Razz the *Culinarian of the Year*, also in 1996. *Gourmet* magazine placed Razz as one of the top twenty restaurants of 1998 in Arizona. More recently, the restaurant received accolades as the *Best Fine Dining Restaurant – Scottsdale* by the *Valley Guide*, and received *Food & Lifestyles* Golden Plate Award as *Most Romantic Restaurant*.

With his dark ponytail, charming smile, and rich, exotic voice, Razz is the charismatic soul of his restaurant. His engaging personality adds a special energy to the dining room as he chats with his guests in between his duties in the bustling open kitchen. The sleek and sophisticated restaurant displays a beautiful gallery of contemporary art, as guests enjoy dishes from around the world. Known nationally for his 5,000 square foot terraced "Chef's Garden," flourishing among the desert landscape, Razz's cuisine features herbs, edible flowers, and exotic fruits and vegetables that are his trademark.

Chef Razz attended the National Hotel School of Lausanne in Switzerland and, after completing his training, moved to the United States and enrolled in the Culinary Institute of America in New York. A native of Venezuela, he is the seventh generation of chefs in his family. Before opening his own restaurant, he was the Chef de Cuisine at Etiennes Different Pointe of View at The Pointe Hilton at Tapatio Cliffs, Phoenix.

A favorite guest of the *Food Network*, Chef Razz has also appeared on other television broadcasts of *Ready-Set-Cook, Chef du Jour, Dining Around*, and *Talking Food with Robin Leach*. Locally, he has a regularly televised spot called *Cooking Under Ten*, which features restaurant-quality recipes that can be prepared in less than ten minutes for fewer than ten dollars.

Razz and Bobbi Jo give back to the community, as do so many chefs, by participating in many culinary events for charity. They are also members of the culinary advisory board for Metro Tech of Phoenix, a vocational institute with a culinary arts program for at-risk high school students.

Green Papaya Salad

Ingredients

4   ounces pork loin, chopped
4   ounces shrimp, cleaned, chopped
1   teaspoon olive oil
1½ teaspoons chile paste
1   teaspoon garlic, peeled, chopped
1   medium carrot, julienned
1   medium onion, julienned
1   stalk celery, julienned
2   limes, juice of
4   tablespoons palm sugar or honey
2   tablespoons lemongrass paste (or 3
     tablespoons lemongrass syrup, but
     omit palm sugar/honey)

3   tablespoons tamarind juice
3   tablespoons light olive oil
4   cups unripe papaya, peeled, cleaned,
     julienned
1   medium firm tomato, diced
1½ teaspoons cilantro, finely chopped
1½ teaspoons basil, finely chopped
1½ teaspoons mint, finely chopped
1½ teaspoons parsley, finely chopped
¼   cup green bean vermicelli noodles,
     softened in hot water
salt and pepper to taste

Preparation

IN A saucepan, sauté the pork and shrimp in olive oil. Add chile paste, garlic, carrot, onion, and celery. Stir over medium heat and add the lime juice, palm sugar, lemongrass paste, tamarind juice, and light olive oil. Transfer the warm ingredients to a mixing bowl. Add papaya, tomato, cilantro, basil, mint, and parsley, and toss together. Finish by adding the softened green bean vermicelli noodles and season to taste with salt and pepper.

Serves 4

Salmon Spring Roll Salad

Ingredients

2 6-ounce salmon filets, cut into thin
   strips
2 small carrots, peeled & julienned
2 stalks celery, julienned
2 leeks, julienned
2 red peppers, julienned
1 cup radish sprouts
1 teaspoon chili paste

1 tablespoon soy sauce
2 limes, juice from
8 egg roll wrappers
1 egg, beaten
1½ cup oil
   salt and pepper to taste
   Salad (recipe follows)

Preparation

IN A mixing bowl, toss the salmon strips, carrots, celery, leeks, red peppers, radish sprouts, chili paste, soy sauce, and lime juice, and set aside. Lay a sheet of egg roll wrapper flat and moisten the edges of it with the beaten egg. Place ¼ of the vegetable and salmon mix on 1 corner of the wrapper. Start rolling tight to halfway, then fold the ends towards the middle, and finish rolling until completely secured. Fry the spring rolls in hot oil until golden in color.

PLACE the salad greens in the center of 4 plates. Cut the spring rolls in half diagonally and place 4 halves around each plate.

Serves 4

For the Salad

4 cups salad mixed baby lettuces,
   chopped
2 tablespoons onion, chopped
1 teaspoon chili paste
1 teaspoon sesame oil

4 tablespoons honey
4 tablespoons lime juice
4 tablespoons olive oil
2 tablespoons water
   salt and pepper to taste.

TOSS all ingredients together and season with salt and pepper to taste. Reserve for serving.

Sassi
Ristorante

SASSI

10455 E. Pinnacle Peak Parkway
Scottsdale, AZ 85255
480-502-9095
www.sassi.biz

Dinner Tuesday through Sunday
starting at 5:30pm

Sassi Ristorante

Kevin and Sharon Walsh, Owners
Wade Moises, Executive Chef
Stephen Plunkett, General Manager

Opened in February 2004, Sassi Ristorante is a spectacular re-creation of a southern Italian villa in its entire splendor. Owners Kevin and Sharon Walsh spent several years planning the architectural construction and the ambience that they wanted to achieve. Their dream was to create a destination restaurant with a comfortable, residential feel in the serene setting of the Sonora Desert. They chose Italian food because, as Kevin likes to say, "what other cuisine can someone eat more than once a week". General Manager Stephen Plunkett, a Culinary Institute of America graduate, contributed design and operational ideas based on his more than twenty years as a chef, manager, and consultant in the restaurant, hotel, and private club business. Kevin and Sharon added their design ideas from their travels to Italy and their thoughts about comfort and service in restaurants.

With the theme of Italian food for the restaurant, Wade Moises was hired as Executive Chef. Wade, also a graduate of the Culinary Institute of America, he had assisted in the planning and opening of Mario Batali's Lupa Osteria Romana in New York City, where he served as Sous Chef/Chef di Cuisine. Before opening Sassi, Wade spent time in Italy gathering ideas and cooking in a small trattoria in Avellino, in the province of Puglia, as well as spending time with friends at their olive oil producing estate in Sicily. Sassi's menu is built around the rustic dishes inspired by his meals in Puglia, Sicily, Campagnia, Basilicata, and other areas in southern Italy. The wine list features a mostly Italian selection of wines from southern Italy and numerous additional wines from Tuscany, Veneto, and Peimonte. Keeping with the relaxed ambience intended by the owners, wine service is less formal, with a wine steward offering assistance and suggestions but without the formal attire or silver tasting cup that can intimidate diners.

The thoughtful design of Sassi offers different dining rooms for different occasions or desires. The Ristorante will try to accommodate guests in the room of their choice. The Kitchen Dining Room has a cozy, informal feel. In this room, diners can get a glimpse of the energetic bustle of the kitchen staff, and there is also a European style community dining table ideal for solo diners or walk-in guests. The Garden Terrace offers captivating views of the city lights and surrounding mountains, while The Library provides more intimate dining. The Main Dining Room features a freestanding limestone fireplace, wood flooring, and large, oversized furniture.

INSALATA DI AGRUMI

Fresh Citrus Salad

Ingredients

1 grapefruit
1 lemon
1 tangerine
1 orange
   honey, as needed
   salt and pepper to taste

extra virgin olive oil
1 fennel bulb, shaved thin
1 bunch arugula
2 ounces shaved pecorino cheese
2 teaspoons bee pollen

Preparation

REMOVE the rinds from the grapefruit, lemon, tangerine, and orange. Then segment or slice them, saving any juice in a small bowl as you go. Add to the saved juice a teaspoon or two of honey, salt and pepper, and a few tablespoons of olive oil. Toss the fennel, arugula, and citrus segments together. Add the citrus juice dressing as needed to coat the salad, then season with salt and pepper. Place the salad on a plate, top with shaved pecorino cheese, and then sprinkle with bee pollen.

Serves 2

Linguini Cedro
Linguini Pasta with Lemon

Ingredients

8 *ounces linguini pasta*

2 *ounces butter*

2 *ounces extra virgin olive oil*

2 *ounces Meyer lemon juice*

4 *slices Meyer lemon*

Preparation

BRING 1 gallon of salted water to a boil. Place the pasta in the boiling water.

IN A sauté pan, place butter, olive oil, lemon juice, lemon slices, and a splash of the pasta cooking water to gently melt the butter. When the pasta is cooked to desired doneness, place the pasta in the sauté pan, cook for 1 minute with the lemon sauce and toss well. Adjust the consistency of your sauce with a few splashes of pasta water if necessary.

Serves 2

Wine suggestion: A light white wine with crisp citrus flavors. A perfect match might be an Inzolia/ Chardonnay blend from Sicily. Inzolia is an indigenous grape in Sicily and contributes the crispness and floral aromas. The wine is aged in stainless steel, not oak, so it does not have the buttery-vanilla or oaky flavors of an American wine. Also try Bidini Bidis or Cusamano Angimbe.

Spaghetti alla Carbonara

Ingredients

4 ounces spaghetti pasta
1 ounce olive oil
1-2 ounces guanciale or pancetta
    black pepper to taste

1 ounce butter
1 scallion, sliced
1 egg
2 ounces pecorino cheese

Preparation

IN A pot of boiling salted water, begin to cook the pasta. Meanwhile, in a sauté pan add olive oil and guanciale and cook over low heat until the guanciale is brown and crispy. Add pepper to taste and then add 2 ounces of pasta water to the pan to stop the cooking. Remove the pan from the heat and then add the butter. Remove the pasta from the water 1 minute before done and add it to the pan. Return the pan to a medium flame and add a little more pasta water. Toss the pasta with the guanciale. Allowing the guanciale and pasta to cook together will develop the best possible flavor and consistency. Now, for the finishing touch, add another few ounces of pasta water and then add the scallions and the egg. Toss the egg very well with the pasta and allow to cook for about 20 seconds. Remove the pan from the heat and continue tossing. If the pasta appears to be sticking to the pan, add pasta water to "lube" it up until the pasta slides off the bottom of the pan and makes the slightest slapping sound on it. Add the pecorino, toss one more time, and serve.

Serves 1

Wine suggestion: Drink a Sangiovese-based wine from Tuscany, such as a Chianti Classico, or Chianti Rufina, or a Carmignano which is a predominantly Sangiovese wine with a small percentage of Cabernet.

POLPETTINI
Meatballs

Ingredients

2 pounds 20% fat ground beef, well
  chilled
4 tablespoons salt
4 teaspoons ground black pepper
4 teaspoons sugar
2 teaspoons ground cayenne
4 fresh sage leaves, chopped
2 teaspoons rosemary, chopped fine
¼ cup parsley leaves, chopped
6 cloves garlic, minced, divided

½ cup breadcrumbs
½ cup milk
2 onions
3 tablespoons olive oil
  salt and pepper to taste
2 cups white wine
1 lemon, juice from
2 bay leaves
4 thin lemon slices, for garnish
¼ cup whole parsley leaves, for garnish

Preparation

HEAT the oven to 325 degrees. Combine beef, salt, pepper, sugar, cayenne, sage, rosemary, parsley, 4 cloves of the garlic, breadcrumbs, and milk, and mix by hand until sticky and homogenous, but not warm. Make 1 small ball and cook through to do a taste test. If necessary, re-season the mixture. Form into 2-ounce balls and place on a lipped baking sheet. Dampen or oil your hands while forming balls, to help make them smooth and evenly shaped. Roast in the oven until golden brown, about 15-20 minutes.

HEAT the oven to 300 degrees. On a range-top, in an ovenproof pot, sweat onions and remaining 2 cloves of garlic in olive oil until soft and clear. Season well with salt and pepper and deglaze with white wine. Add lemon juice, bay leaves, and cooked meatballs with all their pan juices into the pot and place it in the oven. Braise for about 1 to 1½ hours or until tender. Garnish with lemon slices and whole parsley leaves.

Serves 4

Wine suggestion: A light red without too much tannin, since the tannin would not be a good match for the pepper in the meatballs. A good suggestion might be a Primitivo, a jammy, robust wine without too much tannin. Primitivo is the same grape known in the U.S. as Zinfandel, which would also be a good choice. A-Mano makes a good Primitivo in Puglia.

SPIEDINI DI MANZO
Skewered Beef

Ingredients

1 tablespoon rosemary, chopped	10 cherry tomatoes
3 cloves garlic, chopped	2 skewers
4 tablespoons extra virgin olive oil,	salt and pepper to taste
divided	4 ounces arugula
1 8-ounce beef tenderloin, cut into 10	2 ounces Parmesan cheese, shaved
small cubes	1 Meyer lemon, cut into wedges

Preparation

HEAT a grill. Combine rosemary and garlic with 2 tablespoons of the olive oil and toss with the cubed beef and cherry tomatoes. Next, place the beef and tomatoes in alternating sequence on 2 skewers. Season to taste with salt and pepper. Grill the skewers to desired doneness. Toss arugula with the remaining olive oil, season with salt and pepper to taste, and lay on a plate. Place the grilled skewers over the arugula and top with Parmesan cheese. Finish with a squeeze of Meyer lemon.

Serves 2

Wine suggestion: Try a Nero D'Avola. This is an indigenous grape of Sicily, grown there for over 1,000 years. It makes a full bodied, slightly spicy wine that is soft and easy to drink. Try looking for Donnafugata or Carlo Hauner for delicious wines from this grape.

Quail hunters in Oracle.

elements

at Sanctuary on
Camelback Mountain

elements

5700 East McDonald Drive
Paradise Valley, AZ 85253
480-607-2300
www.sanctuaryoncamelback.com

Open Daily for Breakfast, Lunch,
and Dinner
Also Serving Sunday Brunch

elements at Sanctuary on Camelback Mountain

Beau MacMillan, Executive Chef
Peter Juneja, Restaurant Manager

There is a magical otherworldly quality about Sanctuary on Camelback Mountain, set in Phoenix's Paradise Valley. The lush green of the landscaping with its towering palm trees is in stark contrast to the red rocks of Camelback Mountain. This lavish 58-acre resort offers private homes, casitas, and suites for the discriminating traveler. A member of Small Luxury Hotels of the World, Sanctuary is a AAA Four-Diamond resort. Five champion tennis courts and a luxurious spa complete the amenities. But, one of the best restaurants in the Phoenix area is at the heart of the resort.

elements is a strikingly handsome restaurant with a sophisticated décor and a creative menu. The seating is comfortable and orients the guests to the outdoors with panoramic windows framing a spectacular view of Paradise Valley. A "family style" table slices through the middle of the room, giving guests the opportunity to dine with other guests. An outdoor dining area with outdoor heating arrangements allows al fresco dining for many months of the year. The jade bar abuts the restaurant, sharing its views, and offering a lively gathering place before or after dinner, and the outdoor bar patio has a fire bowl as its centerpiece on cool evenings. *Wine Spectator* has awarded the restaurant its *Award of Excellence* for its superb wine list.

Executive Chef Beau MacMillan inspires his staff with his passion for fresh, local ingredients many of which are procured from a network of artisans and organic farmers. A native of Plymouth, Massachusetts, he is a graduate of Johnson and Wales University in Providence, Rhode Island. After serving as the Sous Chef at La Vielle Maison in Boca Raton, Florida, Chef MacMillan was drawn to the culinary scene on the West Coast, where, among other positions, he was the Sous Chef at the prestigious Hotel Bel Air. He was recruited to Arizona in 1998 to develop the cuisine at The Ranch on Camelback, which later became Sanctuary on Camelback Mountain. Chef MacMillan and former Executive Chef Charles Wiley opened elements in March 2001.

Now as Executive Chef, he has brought national recognition to the restaurant. In March 2006, Chef MacMillan was invited to *The Food Network's* kitchen stadium to compete against Iron Chef Bobby Flay in the hit series, *Iron Chef America*, in the "Battle of American Kobe Beef". Chef MacMillan's cuisine reigned supreme and he was declared the winner over Chef Flay. Chef MacMillan has also been a featured chef at The James Beard House and at Bon Appetit magazine in New York, and regularly conducts cooking classes for the guests of Sanctuary.

elements

142

 Award of Excellence

Kobe Beef Carpaccio

Chef Beau MacMillan and his staff used this dish when they competed, and won, on "Iron Chef America."

Ingredients

4 ounces American Kobe beef tenderloin
2 ounces organic greens
1 small carrot, julienned
1 small green papaya, julienned
1 small red onion, julienned

2 scallions, chopped
1 avocado, sliced
  Soy Drizzle (recipe follows)
1 lotus root, sliced

Preparation

SLICE the beef as thin as possible. Place each slice between 2 pieces of plastic wrap and lightly pound until the meat is even and thin. Place it on a plate and refrigerate. Place the greens in a small bowl with the carrot, papaya, and onion. Drizzle a small amount of Soy Drizzle on the salad.

REMOVE beef carpaccio from refrigerator. Line a plate with avocado and scallion. Place salad in the center of the carpaccio and garnish the plate with 2 tablespoons of Soy Drizzle. Lightly fry the lotus chips until they are crisp and garnish the salad with them.

Serves 2

Wine suggestion: Cabernet Sauvignon or Merlot

For the Soy Drizzle

⅓ cup soy sauce
⅓ cup rice wine vinegar
⅓ cup scallions, green parts only, sliced
  ⅛ inch thick

1 tablespoon toasted sesame oil
1 tablespoon sambal oelek

COMBINE all ingredients in a medium bowl and stir to blend.

Yield: 1 cup

HEIRLOOM TOMATOES
with Mozzarella and Basil

This item is featured on our summer menu. All the ingredients are from local Arizona organic farmers.

Ingredients

3 whole heirloom tomatoes, medium size
1 lobe fresh buffalo mozzarella
3 whole heirloom tomatoes, small size
1 teaspoon basil oil

1 bundle fresh basil
1 pinch sea salt
   Balsamic Chili Glaze (recipe follows)
   basil pesto crostini, for garnish

Preparation

SLICE mozzarella and large tomatoes ¼ inch thick. Cut smaller tomatoes in half and cover with basil oil. Chiffonade the basil and add it to the small tomatoes. Season with sea salt. Place 1 sliced tomato in the center of the plate and place the sliced mozzarella on top. Continue process until there are 3 slices of each in a circle. Place small tomatoes and basil around the outside of the plate. Drizzle with Balsamic Chili Glaze and season with sea salt. Garnish the plate with a basil pesto crostini.

Yield: 1 small platter

Wine suggestion: Pinot Noir or Sauvignon Blanc.

For the Balsamic Chili Glaze

½ ounce olive oil
⅛ ounce garlic, chopped
⅛ ounce shallot, chopped
1 sprig fresh thyme

1 pinch chili flakes
2 cups balsamic vinegar
1 cup honey

HEAT oil in a saucepan over medium heat. Sweat garlic, shallot, chili flakes, and thyme. Stir and deglaze with vinegar. Reduce mixture by half and add honey. Cook 5 minutes and chill.

Yield: 2 cups

LOBSTER AND ROCK SHRIMP FRITTER

Anything with lobster in it is Chef Beau MacMillan's specialty, as he is a New England native.

Ingredients

½ cup rock shrimp
2 ounces poached lobster, chilled &
    chopped
1 egg
1 ounce heavy cream

3 scallions, chopped
⅛ teaspoon Old Bay seasoning
½ cup panko Japanese crumbs
    tarragon aioli, to accompany

Preparation

PLACE shrimp, lobster, egg, and heavy cream in a robo coupe until the mixture is smooth. Fold in scallions and season with the Old Bay. Divide into 2 parts and dredge each in the Japanese breadcrumbs. Sauté on medium heat for 2 minutes on each side. Serve with tarragon aioli.

Serves 2

Wine suggestion: Sauvignon Blanc or Chardonnay.

elements

CHILLED LOBSTER TIAN

Ingredients

1¼ pounds Maine lobster
    Court Bouillon (recipe follows)
2 ounces buckwheat noodles
½ ounce spinach
1 scallion
4 leaves basil
4 leaves mint
2 tablespoons Sesame Aioli, divided
    (recipe follows)

1 tablespoon basil oil
1 tablespoon chili oil
¼ avocado
1 ounce mango, diced
½ ounce micro greens
2 slices lotus root
1 ounce fried wonton
1 pinch sesame seeds

Preparation

POACH the lobster in the Court Bouillon. Then remove it and place it in an ice bath. Remove lobster meat from shell and chill. Cook the buckwheat noodles according to package directions and cool them. Chop basil and mint and add to noodles. Chop spinach and scallions and add to noodles. Season noodles with 1 tablespoon of the sesame aioli.

ON A large plate, place the remaining tablespoon of Sesame Aioli in a circular motion in the center of the plate. Drizzle the plate with basil oil and chili oil. Place a tian mold, or other individual shallow earthenware casserole, in the center of the plate and fill with the noodle mixture, pressing down so noodles are firm. Place lobster meat and avocado on top of the noodles. Garnish with mango, micro greens, lotus root slices, crisp wonton, and sesame seeds.

Serves 1

For the Court Bouillon

1 gallon water
1 cup white wine
½ teaspoon peppercorns
1 bay leaf
1 sprig thyme
1 lemon, halved

1 leek, split and washed
1 carrot
1 onion
1 celery stalk
2 cloves garlic
1 ounce kosher salt

COMBINE all ingredients in a large saucepot and bring to a slow simmer.

For the Sesame Aioli

2 tablespoons olive oil	5 ounces rice wine vinegar
1 jalapeño, diced	5 ounces mirin
2 shallots, finely	13½ ounces tamari or soy sauce
2½ cups fresh ginger, minced	7½ ounces sesame oil
¼ cup garlic, minced	1 gallon mayonnaise

HEAT olive oil in a small skillet. Add jalapeño, shallot, ginger, and garlic and sauté over medium heat. Remove from pan and place in bowl. Add vinegar, mirin, and tamari and slowly whisk in sesame oil. Allow mixture to cool and then add mayonnaise, whisking until smooth.

Dutch oven cooking in Oracle.

LON's
at the Hermosa

LONs
at the hermosa

5532 N. Palo Cristi Road
Paradise Valley, AZ 85253
602-955-7878
www.lons.com
www.hermosainn.com

Lunch Served Monday through Friday
11:30am – 2:00pm
Dinner Served Nightly
6:00pm – 10:00pm
Sunday Jazz Brunch
10:00am – 2:00pm

LON's at the Hermosa

Michael Rusconi, Executive Chef

Cowboy artist, Alonzo "Lon" Megargee, came West from Philadelphia in the early 20th century, setting up a studio and home in the wide-open desert that has now become a part of Paradise Valley. He used adobe blocks and old wood and beams from an abandoned mine for the structure and dubbed his home "Casa Hermosa", or "beautiful house." To supplement his art income, he began running Casa Hermosa as a guest ranch. In 1941, in the midst of a divorce and short of money, Lon put his property on the market. The new owners, planning to use the property as their private residence, were surprised late one night by a taxi-full of guests, and soon found themselves in the guest ranch business. Over the years, the Inn evolved with the addition of a pool, tennis courts, and the casitas and villas. But, by the late 1980s, the resort was caught in the financial crunch in most of the West, and a devastating fire in 1987 damaged the main building. In 1992, Fred and Jennifer Unger purchased the property and worked tirelessly to restore its original charm, saving the fire-damaged building, restoring the charred old beams, and cleaning up the original ironwork.

Today, LON's occupies most of that main building and the beautiful adobe-walled garden patio. The elegant main dining room displays a warm, yet sophisticated environment with subtle lighting and impeccably set tables. On soft, desert evenings guests enjoy dining on the beautiful patio with soft lighting and flames from the fire pit casting shadows on the adobe walls. The sumptuous culinary selections are complemented by an extensive wine list that has won the *Award of Excellence* from the *Wine Spectator* magazine.

In 2005, Michael Rusconi, joined LON's as Executive Chef, responsible for all food operations of the resort. Chef Rusconi earned his culinary degree from the New England Culinary Institute in Vermont. He moved to the Phoenix area in 1986 to intern with the James Beard award-winning chef Vincent Guerithault. He later worked under another James Beard award winning chef Alex Stratta at Mary Elaine's at the Phoenician Resort and joined the team at the Royal Palms Resort as Executive Sous Chef in 2001. At LON's Chef Rusconi utilizes high quality suppliers to bring in those ingredients not found locally. A cornucopia of organic herbs and heirloom vegetables, fruits, and grains are grown on the premises in the chef's garden, a half-acre site north of the property's kitchens, and used along with the produce of local growers.

Y Award of Excellence

Yellow Gazpacho Soup

Ingredients

30 yellow tomatoes, seeded
15 English cucumbers, peeled and seeded
14 yellow bell peppers, seeded
 1 yellow onion, diced
 1 bunch celery, chopped (no leaves)

 5 zucchini, peeled
 1 tablespoon garlic, chopped
 6 ounces olive oil
10 ounces sherry vinegar
 ¼ bunch cilantro

Preparation

BLEND all ingredients and strain through a medium strainer and serve.

Yield: about 2 gallons

Sweet Potato Soup
with Peppers and Roasted Corn

Ingredients

2 tablespoons butter
1 onion, chopped
1 poblano chile, small diced
1 yellow bell pepper, small diced
1 red bell pepper, small diced
1 tablespoon garlic, chopped

5 ears roasted corn, kernels removed
    from cob
2 large sweet potatoes, small diced
1 tablespoon cilantro, chopped
   water
   salt and pepper to taste

Preparation

PLACE butter in a saucepot and sweat onion, chile, bell peppers, and garlic on low heat until tender. Add corn, sweet potatoes, and cilantro. Cover with water and simmer until all the ingredients are tender. Blend half of the soup in a blender until smooth. Add the blended ingredients back into the remaining soup. Season with salt and pepper.

Yield: about 2 quarts

Roasted Chicken and Strawberry Salad
with Prickly Pear Vinaigrette

Ingredients

6 ounces roasted pulled chicken
4 ounces fresh mozzarella, diced
1 pint fresh strawberries, quartered
  baby field greens

3 ounces toasted almonds
Prickly Pear Vinaigrette
  (recipe follows)

Preparation

TOSS chicken, mozzarella, strawberries, and greens together. Add Prickly Pear Vinaigrette and toss again. Place in a bowl and garnish with the toasted almonds.

Serves 1

Wine suggestion: Champagne

For the Prickly Pear Vinaigrette

1 ounce shallot, chopped
½ fresh pear, peeled & quartered
2 ounces white balsamic vinegar
2 ounces prickly pear syrup

4 ounces olive oil, plus some to sauté
1 ice cube
  salt and white pepper to taste

SWEAT shallot and quartered pear in olive oil, and then let them cool. In a blender, combine the cooked pear mixture, balsamic vinegar, and prickly pear syrup. Blend until smooth. Slowly add the 4 ounces of olive oil. As the vinaigrette starts to thicken, add the ice cube. This will keep the vinaigrette cold and help keep it from getting too thick as it is being blended. Add salt and white pepper to taste, and reserve for serving.

MARINATED LOBSTER AND SCALLOPS IN JICAMA TORTILLA

Ingredients

2 fresh 1½-pound Maine lobsters
1 pound dry-packed scallops
¾ cup lime juice
¼ cup olive oil
½ teaspoon fine sea salt
1 jalapeño, seeded and diced small
¼ red bell pepper, diced small
¼ yellow bell pepper, diced small

½ stalk celery, diced small
¼ red onion, diced small
1 tablespoon cilantro, chopped
1 large jicama, peeled and sliced thin
   blanched chives for garnish
   garden greens
   Cilantro Lime Dressing (recipe follows)

Preparation

BLANCH lobsters in a large pot of boiling water for 3 minutes. Cool lobsters in ice water, then split them with a chef's knife. Pull out all the lobster meat and slice into small medallions. Place in a medium-sized mixing bowl.

CLEAN the connector muscle from the side of the scallop. Slice them very thinly and add to the lobsters in the bowl. Add lime juice, olive oil, salt, jalapeño, bell peppers, celery, onion, cilantro, and jicama. Allow to marinate for 4 hours or until the translucency has disappeared from the scallops. The acid in the lemon juice will cook them.

TO SERVE, lay a thin slice of jimaca on a cutting board. Fill with the marinated seafood and vegetable mix. Fold the filled jimaca like a taco and tie with a blanched chive. Serve over garden greens dressed with the Cilantro Lime Dressing.

Serves 4 – 6

Wine suggestion: Sauvignon Blanc

For the Cilantro Lime Dressing

2 tablespoons cilantro, chopped
¼ cup lime juice
1 teaspoon honey

¼ cup olive oil
1 shallot
   sea salt and white pepper to taste

PLACE cilantro, lime juice, and honey in a blender and blend. On medium speed, slowly blend in the oil. Finish with salt and pepper. This dressing is only a temporary emulsion, so use immediately.

GEORGES BANK SEA SCALLOPS
with Black Truffle Spätzle, Lemon Butter Sauce, and Organic Spinach

Ingredients

10 sea scallops, 10 – 20 count
    sea salt and white pepper to taste
    clarified butter to sauté
¼ pound spinach

olive oil to sauté
Black Truffle Spätzle (recipe follows)
Lemon Butter Sauce (recipe follows)
micro amaranth for garnish

Preparation

SEASON scallops with salt and white pepper. Sauté them in clarified butter in a frying pan on very high heat for about 5 minutes. The scallops should brown slightly and lose their translucency. Wash and clean the spinach. In a hot sauté pan, quickly sauté the spinach in olive oil. Season with salt and pepper.

TO SERVE, place a small pile of spinach in the middle of 2 large dinner plates. Place a small pile of Black Truffle Spätzle over the spinach. Place 5 scallops per plate around the spaetzle and drizzle the Lemon Butter Sauce around the outside. Garnish with a little micro amaranth and serve immediately.

Serves 2

For the Black Truffle Spätzle

2½ cups all purpose flour
 5 eggs
 1 tablespoon truffle oil
 ½ cup whole milk

2 large black truffles, chopped fine
   salt and pepper to taste
   olive oil to coat

MIX flour into the eggs. Add milk, olive oil, truffles, and a touch of salt. Scrape the mix through a large perforated pan or colander into boiling water. Once spätzle floats to the top, remove immediately. Shock the spätzle in ice water, then lightly oil with olive oil to prevent it from sticking together. To serve, reheat in whole butter, browning it lightly. Finish with salt and pepper.

For the Lemon Butter Sauce

1 shallot, chopped
1 lemon, zest and juice from
½ pound unsalted butter, small cubes,
    divided

½ cup white wine
2 tablespoons heavy cream
   sea salt to taste
   ground white pepper to taste

IN A small saucepot on low heat, sweat shallot and lemon zest in 1 tablespoon of the butter until translucent. Add the white wine and reduce it until almost dry. Add cream and lemon juice and very slowly whisk in the butter over low heat. Do not add the butter too quickly or the sauce will become too cold and separate. Reserve for serving.

Wine suggestion: Pinot Gris

Ancho Honey Glazed American Salmon

with Grilled Fennel, Roasted Fingerling Potatoes, Tomato Tarragon Jus, and Fava Beans

Ingredients

- 1½ pounds fingerling potatoes (red B's may be substituted)
- 2 tablespoons olive oil, divided olive oil for sautéing
- 1 tablespoon garlic, finely chopped
- ¼ teaspoon sea salt, plus to taste
- ⅛ teaspoon ground black pepper, plus to taste

- 2 bulbs fennel, sliced in large pieces
- 32 fava beans
- 1 teaspoon lemon juice
- 1 teaspoon Ancho chile flakes
- 4 ounces orange blossom honey
- 4 6-ounce salmon filets
  Tomato Tarragon Jus (recipe follows)

Preparation

HEAT the oven to 350 degrees. Toss potatoes with 1 tablespoon of olive oil, garlic, ¼ teaspoon of salt, and ⅛ teaspoon pepper. Roast in the oven until tender. Fingerlings take about 15 – 20 minutes and red B's take a little longer. Reserve warm for serving.

TOSS the fennel in the remaining tablespoon of olive oil, and salt and pepper to season. Grill on a barbecue until tender. Reserve for serving.

QUICKLY blanch fava beans for 20 seconds in rapidly boiling water. Cool them and remove the outer shell of the beans. Quickly sauté them in a frying pan with a little olive oil and salt and pepper. Reserve warm for serving.

COMBINE lemon juice, ancho chile flakes, and honey in a small pot. Bring to a boil and take off the stove. Lightly oil the salmon and season it with a little salt and pepper. Grill it on a very hot grill until almost completely done. Brush on the honey glaze and allow it to caramelize on the grill. Be careful not to burn it. The glaze will darken quickly.

TO SERVE, plate the salmon, potatoes, fennel, and fava beans with the Tomato Tarragon Jus.

Serves 4

For the Tomato Tarragon Jus

- 2 roma tomatoes, cored
- 8 ounces chicken stock

- 1 tablespoon fresh tarragon
- ¼ cup extra virgin olive oil

ROAST tomatoes on a barbecue grill. Allow them to cool and then peel the skin off, cut them in half, and squeeze out the seeds. Bring the chicken stock to a boil in a saucepot. In a large blender, blend tomatoes, chicken stock, and tarragon. Slowly blend in the olive oil and season to taste. Reserve warm for serving.

Wine suggestion: Light to medium-bodied Pinot Noir

ALMOND MACAROONS

Ingredients

4 cups almond paste

2 cups granulated sugar

2 cups confectioner's sugar

1¼ cup egg whites

Preparation

IN A stand mixer with the paddle attachment, break up the almond paste. Add granulated sugar slowly, and then add confectioner's sugar slowly. Shut mixer off and scrape the sides of the bowl so that all of the almond paste is incorporated. Turn mixer on speed 1 and slowly stream in the egg whites. When they are added, turn the mixer on speed 2 and beat for 20 seconds. Turn the mixer off and remove from the stand.

HEAT the oven to 350 degrees. Place the batter in a large cloth piping bag with a ¼ inch plain tip. Pipe batter in rows on parchment-lined baking sheets, allowing an inch around each cookie. Before placing them in the oven, tap the cookies with a damp towel. This will give them their signature crackle. Bake for 12 – 15 minutes until light and golden. Allow them to cool on the pans. These cookies can be kept in the freezer for 1 week, but they are best the day they are made. Enjoy!

Yield: 32 2-ounce cookies

LON's at the Hermosa

Christopher's Fermier Brasserie
Paola's Wine Bar

Christopher Gross, Executive Chef/Owner
Paola Embry Gross, Director of Wine/Owner

Opened in October 1998, Christopher's Fermier Brasserie (farmer's tavern) welcomes all those who enjoy fresh food meticulously prepared and presented, with many ingredients obtained from the top local and regional farmers. Many of the dishes are prepared in the wood-burning oven. The cuisine is French inspired, keeping simplicity in mind. Step up to the expansive covered porch, where guests can enjoy dining al fresco, and enter the restaurant through the beautiful glass-paned wood door that sports a large spoon as the handle. Inside, the high-ceilinged restaurant is sleekly contemporary, yet imparts the ambience of a friendly country tavern.

Christopher Gross honed his culinary skills in London and France, as well as some prestigious restaurants in the United States. His first joint venture was Le Relais, where he was able to close the restaurant in the summer in order to travel to France to continue learning new culinary techniques. In 1990, he opened Christopher's, an elegant French-inspired dining room, and Christopher's Bistro, a more casual dining room featuring American International cuisine with a French flair. Both restaurants received many accolades from the culinary press, as well as the *Best of Award of Excellence* from the *Wine Spectator*. In 1995, the James Beard Foundation named Christopher *Best Chef in the Southwest* and in 1997, he was the first chef to receive the *Robert Mondavi Culinary Award of Excellence*.

In 1992, Paola Embry, a native of Chile, joined the team as the Wine Director for the two restaurants. And, in 1993 she married Christopher, creating a team that is peerless. She has also selected the perfect wine for each item on the restaurant's menu. Her extensive knowledge of wines has garnered her several notable degrees. She has received the *Certificat de Merite* from le Comite National des Vins de France and a *Degree of Honor* from Les Amis de Vin International Wine Society. Most recently, she was one of a select few to be inducted into the prestigious Confrérie des Amis du Bontemps in Bordeaux, France.

Paola's Wine Bar showcases a wine-by-the-glass program that rotates each month. One hundred wines are rotated, with thirty offered each month, one wine each day, to highlight great wines from around the world. A large selection of cigars and private humidors are on hand for the cigar enthusiast. The wine bar also offers a cheese program, as well as specialty platters including seafood, charcuterie, and oysters. Soup, pizza, and desserts are also available, as is a late night menu on weekends.

 Award of Excellence

Wild Mushroom Soup with Foie Gras

Ingredients

6 ounces port
4 cups duck stock
4 ounces chanterelles
4 ounces mushroom caps
1 tablespoon olive oil
1 tablespoon shallots, finely chopped
3 tablespoons fresh tarragon leaves or chervil, coarsely chopped

1 tomato, peeled, seeded, finely diced
12 ounces foie gras
1 piece truffle (winter or summer), grated
1 teaspoon white truffle oil

Preparation

REDUCE the port to 2 ounces (¼ cup). Bring the stock to a boil and add the reduced port and any mushroom stems, peels, or pieces left from cleaning the chanterelles and mushroom caps. Simmer about 5 minutes, then strain and keep hot for serving.

SAUTÉ chanterelles and mushroom caps in the olive oil. Add shallots and continue cooking until shallots are soft and translucent. Place the mushrooms, tarragon, and tomato in the bottom of 8 shallow soup bowls.

SAUTÉ the foie gras in a very hot pan on both sides until desired temperature. Place it on top of the mushroom mixture in the center of each bowl. Place the grated truffle around this mixture in the bowl, and then pour in the soup. Spoon a drop of truffle oil into each bowl and serve.

Serves 8

Wine suggestion: Veuve Clicquot Ponsardin, Gold Label, France

Whitefish with Tomato Tea and Fresh Herbs

Ingredients

1 pound whitefish
    salt and pepper to taste
6 large, ripe tomatoes

1 clove garlic
½ cup fresh herbs, fine chopped (chervil, tarragon, basil, etc.)

Preparation

CUT fish into 4 equal portions of 4 ounces each, season with salt and pepper, and keep refrigerated. Using a blender, extract the juice from the tomatoes and garlic. Place the juice in a saucepan and simmer over medium high heat until it reduces by half. As the juice is reducing, gently remove the red tomato mousse that is forming at the top and reserve. Set the mousse on top of a coffee filter to help remove additional liquid. Using soup spoons, form quenelles from the mousse for garnish.

HEAT oven broiler and broil fish it reaches the desired temperature. Place the fish into a shallow bowl and pour tomato broth on top. Garnish with the mousse quenelles and fresh herbs. (The tomato broth is also great for bloody Mary martinis by shaking it with 4 ounces of vodka.)

Serves 4

Wine suggestion: Drylands Sauvignon Blanc, Marlborough, New Zealand

Christopher's Fermier Brasserie

Parnassienne au Chocolate
Chocolate Tower with Espresso Sauce

As seen on Julia Child's PBS series, In Julia's Kitchen with Master Chefs with Chef Christopher Gross.

Ingredients

8½ ounces semi-sweet chocolate, broken into pieces, divided

3 tablespoons unsalted butter, sliced

¼ cup heavy cream

1¼ cups egg whites (10 large)

4 tablespoons superfine sugar

6 ounces white chocolate, cut into pieces, melted

Espresso Sauce (recipe follows)

Preparation

POUR 2 inches of water into a saucepan and bring to a slow simmer. Set a stainless steel bowl on top of the pan; add 5½ ounces of the chocolate and the butter. Stir occasionally as the chocolate melts. In about 5 minutes, when it is smooth and lump-free, remove the bowl and let the chocolate cool to room temperature.

POUR the cream into a stainless steel bowl set over ice and water. Beat by hand or with a portable beater, whipping in as much air as possible, until stiff peaks form. In a separate bowl, beat the egg whites to the soft peak stage. Whip in 2 tablespoons of the sugar and continue beating until stiff peaks form, gradually adding the remainder of the sugar as you beat.

WHISK ¼ of the egg white mixture into the cool melted chocolate, and then gradually add the rest. Fold in the cream quickly, deflating as little as possible. Cut a piece of parchment paper into a rectangle 3½ inches wide by 5 inches long. Form into a cylinder approximately 5 inches tall and 1½ inches in diameter. Close the side with a piece of sticky tape and make sure that it stands up straight. Repeat to form 8 cylinders. Fill a pastry bag with the mousse and pipe it into the tubes, leaving a ½-inch space at the top. Drape the tops of the cylinders with a sheet of plastic and place them in the freezer until frozen solid, approximately 1 hour.

FOR decorating the towers, cut eight 5-inch squares out of parchment paper. Fill a decorating cone with the remaining 3 ounces of semi-sweet chocolate, melted in the same manner as above. Drizzle free-form diagonal lines no more than ¼ inch apart in a lattice pattern across each of the parchment squares. As each square is done, lay flat on one of the baking sheets. When they are all finished, put the sheets in the freezer until the chocolate is set, about 5 minutes. Reserve the remaining melted chocolate.

REMOVE one semi-sweet chocolate lattice from the freezer. With an offset spatula, spread 2-3 tablespoons of the melted white chocolate in a very thin layer on top of the lattice, leaving a 1-inch strip uncoated at one side. Scrape off any excess chocolate. Unwrap 1 frozen mousse tower and lay it on top of the white chocolate, parallel to and opposite the uncoated strip. Quickly wrap the parchment lattice around the mousse, handling it as little as possible, and being careful to leave the uncoated flap overlapping. Return each finished tower to the freezer. The papers may be peeled off after 5 minutes and the chocolate lattice will remain in place around the mousse. Then let the mousse defrost in the refrigerator for about an hour. Serve with the Espresso Sauce.

Serves 8

Wine suggestion: Graham's Six-Grape, Portugal

For the Espresso Sauce

1½ cups half and half
½ fragrant vanilla bean (or 1 teaspoon vanilla extract)
6 egg yolks

⅔ cup sugar
1 cup Illy espresso coffee beans (2 ounces)

HEAT the half and half with the vanilla bean until almost at a simmer, then remove from the heat and cover the pan. Meanwhile, start beating the egg yolks with a hand held mixer in a pan until thick and lemon-colored. Gradually beat in the sugar; then slowly blend in ¼ cup of the hot cream to warm the yolks slowly. Blend slowly to minimize air bubbles. Remove the vanilla bean and blend the remaining cream into the yolk mixture. Pour in the espresso beans and set over low heat, stirring slowly and constantly until the mixture is thick enough to coat the back of the spoon. Strain through a fine meshed sieve into a bowl and let it cool. Can be served warm, tepid, or chilled.

The Farm at South Mountain

6106 S. 32nd Street
Phoenix, AZ 85042
www.thefarmatsouthmountain.com

Farm Kitchen open Tuesday through
Sunday 8:00am – 3:00pm
Open September through May
602-276-6360

Morning Glory Café open Tuesday
through Friday 8:00am – Noon
Saturday & Sunday 8:00am – 1:00pm
Open September through May
602-276-8804

Quiessence open Tuesday through
Saturday 5:00pm – 9:00pm
Open all year
602-276-0601

The Farm at South Mountain

Patricia Christofolo, Owner
Gregory LaPrad, Chef de Cuisine

The Farm at South Mountain is a unique concept in fine dining, offering three separate restaurants that each specialize in one meal of the day. Patricia Christofolo, also owner of Santa Barbara Catering Company, is committed to creating foods that reflect the atmosphere of The Farm: fresh, natural, and wholesome.

In the early 1920s Dwight Heard, benefactor of the Heard Museum, acquired a large parcel of land from 7th Avenue to 48th Street, and from the Salt River bed to the foothills of South Mountain in Phoenix. He subdivided the property into two-acre parcels and sold them with the distinct purpose of promoting self-sufficiency. Heard offered one cow and fifty chickens with each purchase. In keeping with the early philosophy, the ten acres just south of Southern and 32nd Street were planted with one hundred pecan trees, and for over forty years were nurtured by a retired cattleman named Skeeter Coverdale. A.Wayne Smith, a well-known landscape architect, purchased the land from Skeeter in 1983. It is his vision that has guided The Farm's over the years.

Along with the three restaurants, the twelve-acre compound comprises a peaceful aromatic haven and garden lifestyle store, an antique shop, a spa retreat, an office with licensed practitioners of naturopathic medicine, and an organic garden, Maya's at the Farm. Maya Dailey grows and sells fresh produce, flowers, and herbs. Many of the organic items grown in the garden are incorporated into the menus of the three restaurants.

The Morning Glory Café is the perfect place to start your day by enjoying a farm-fresh made-to-order breakfast, and served in the open air. The restaurant is surrounded by organic gardens and framed by a backdrop of vibrant morning glories.

At the original restaurant, the Farm Kitchen, baked goods are made from scratch. The menu features homemade soups, sandwiches, salads, and desserts. Lunch is served in picnic baskets and guests dine on the patio or at picnic tables in the pecan grove.

Quiessence Restaurant & Wine Bar features contemporary American farm cuisine inspired by the Farm's organic garden and the changing seasons. This restaurant is now open all year. Chef de Cuisine, Greg LaPrad is deeply committed to using local sources for his ingredients. The pork, beef, and free-range chicken served at the restaurant are all natural, raised without hormones or antibiotics. Chef LaPrad graduated from Johnson & Wales University in Providence, Rhode Island with a Summa Cum Laude distinction. He has traveled extensively throughout Europe and spent a summer in Africa. He also spent time in Italy, working at Il Bottaccio in Tuscany, which is a Relais & Chateaux rated restaurant.

Cocoa Cinnamon Scones

Ingredients

3¾ cups flour
  4 teaspoons baking powder
  1 teaspoon salt
  ½ cup sugar
  ¼ cup cocoa powder
  2 teaspoons cinnamon

¾ pound butter (3 sticks)
1½ cups whipping cream
  ¼ pound chocolate chips
  1 egg white
     granulated sugar, to garnish

Preparation

MIX flour, baking powder, salt, sugar, cocoa powder, and cinnamon. Cut butter into small cubes. Using a pastry cutter, cut the butter into the dry ingredients. Then add cream and chocolate chips. Do not over mix.

HEAT the oven to 350 degrees. Roll dough out on a lightly floured surface to about 1¼ inch thick. Cut out 2½-inch scones using a round cookie cutter until all the dough is used. Brush the top of the scones with egg white and sprinkle with granulated sugar. Bake for 30 minutes.

Serves 20

BEV'S LEMON SCONES

When The Farm at South Mountain opened its doors in 1993, Beverly Breen was our baker. A baking purist, Beverly would arrive each day at 3:00am to start making scones, pecan pies, cookies, and apricot bars. We honor her memory every day with "Bev's Lemon Scones."

Ingredients

4 cups flour	1 lemon, zest from
4 teaspoons baking powder	½ teaspoon lemon extract
1 teaspoon salt	¾ cup whipping cream
¼ cup sugar	1 egg white
1½ cups butter (3 sticks)	granulated sugar to garnish

Preparation

MIX flour, baking powder, salt, and sugar. Cut butter into small cubes. Using a pastry cutter, cut the butter into the dry ingredients. Add lemon zest and extract, and then add cream. Do not over mix.

HEAT oven to 350 degrees. Roll out the dough on a lightly floured surface to about 1¼ inch thick. Cut out 2½-inch scones using a round cookie cutter until all the dough is used. Brush the top of the scones with egg white and sprinkle with granulated sugar. Bake for 30 minutes.

Serves 15

TRIPLEBERRY PRESERVES

Ingredients

1 cup blueberries	½ cup orange juice
1 cup raspberries	1¼ cups sugar
1 cup cranberries	1 lemon, juice and zest from

Preparation

PUT all ingredients in a saucepan over medium heat. Allow the mixture to cook until it begins to thicken and the cranberries have popped. Cool and serve with Bev's Lemon Scones or use to make an excellent peanut butter and jelly sandwich.

Serves 2½ cups

French Toast with Warm Pecan Glaze

Ingredients

4 eggs
½ cup milk
1 tablespoon vanilla
1 teaspoon cinnamon

1 tablespoon butter
8 slices sourdough bread, about 1 inch
   thick
Warm Pecan Glaze (recipe follows)

Preparation

WHISK eggs, milk, vanilla, and cinnamon. Melt butter in a frying pan over medium heat. Dip bread in the egg batter and fry until golden brown on both sides. Arrange 2 slices of French toast on each plate, spoon the Warm Pecan Glaze over the top, and serve. Yum.

Serves 4

For the Warm Pecan Glaze

½ cup brown sugar
½ cup butter (1 stick)
2 cups chopped pecans
3 tablespoons honey

2 teaspoons vanilla
½ cup maple syrup
   sliced bananas (optional)

IN A pan over medium heat, mix brown sugar, butter, pecans, honey, vanilla, and maple syrup until the butter is melted and the sugar is dissolved. Add the sliced bananas if desired. Reserve warm for serving.

Italian Omelette

Ingredients

3 eggs
1 tablespoon butter
2 tablespoons spinach, sautéed

2 tablespoons mushrooms, sautéed
2 tablespoons roasted peppers
2 ounces mozzarella cheese, grated

Preparation

BREAK eggs into a bowl and beat lightly with a fork. Heat butter in an omelette pan over medium heat. After the butter stops foaming, pour in the eggs and cook. Gently lift up around the edges occasionally to let raw egg run underneath. When the eggs have set to the degree that you like, add the filling (spinach, mushrooms, roasted peppers, and cheese) and start rolling the omelette onto itself with a fork or spatula. Tip the pan and roll the omelette onto a plate and serve immediately.

Serves 1

Farm Frittata with Zucchini, Feta, and Onion

Ingredients

3 tablespoons olive oil, divided
¾ pound green and yellow zucchini, diced
¼ teaspoon salt

¼ teaspoon pepper
½ cup green onion, sliced
¾ cup feta, crumbled, divided
8 eggs, slightly beaten

Preparation

HEAT 1 tablespoon of the olive oil in a large skillet over medium heat. Sauté the zucchini with salt and pepper for about 5 minutes or until tender. Whisk green onion, zucchini, and ½ cup of the feta into the eggs.

HEAT the oven to broil. Heat the remaining 2 tablespoons of olive oil in a large ovenproof skillet over medium heat. Pour in the egg mixture and cook, lifting up around the edges occasionally to let raw egg run underneath. Cook until the eggs start to set and the bottom and sides begin to brown, about 5 minutes. Sprinkle remaining ¼ cup of feta over the top and place the skillet under the broiler for about 2 minutes, or until the eggs start to puff and brown. Loosen the edges and bottom of the frittata with a spatula and slide it onto a plate. Slice it into wedges and serve warm or at room temperature.

Serves 4 – 6

BUTTERNUT SQUASH SOUP

Ingredients

2 tablespoons extra virgin olive oil
1 cup onion, diced
¼ cup celery, sliced
¼ cup carrot, sliced
1 cinnamon stick
   salt and pepper to taste
4 cups vegetable stock

½ teaspoon ground coriander
1½ cups roasted butternut squash
½ cup half and half
¼ cup mascarpone cheese, if desired
2 tablespoons toasted pumpkin seeds, if
   desired

Preparation

HEAT olive oil in a large saucepan over medium heat. Add onion, celery, carrot, and cinnamon stick and sauté until soft, about 10 minutes. Season with salt and pepper. Add vegetable stock and coriander and bring to a boil. Simmer for several minutes, and then stir in squash, and simmer for another 10 – 15 minutes to let the flavors meld. Discard cinnamon stick and purée the soup in a blender until smooth. Return the soup to the pan and reheat. Add half and half and additional salt and pepper, if necessary. To serve, garnish with a spoonful of mascarpone and a scattering of pumpkin seeds, if desired.

Serves 4

Hazelnut Pesto Chicken Salad

Ingredients

1 cup hazelnuts
2 cups fresh basil leaves
4 cloves garlic
1 cup Parmesan cheese

½ teaspoon salt
1 cup extra virgin olive oil
4 chicken breasts, cooked and cubed
½ cup mayonnaise

Preparation

HEAT the oven to 350 degrees. To toast the hazelnuts (which removes the brown skins and enhances the flavor), spread the nuts in a single layer on a baking sheet. Bake them for about 15 minutes or until the skins start to dry up and begin to flake off. Then place the nuts on a towel, fold the towel over the nuts, and rub vigorously. Most of the skin will come off. Don't worry if a few little bits of skin remain on the nuts. Pick out the nuts and discard the skins.

MIX the toasted hazelnuts, basil, garlic, Parmesan, and salt in a blender or food processor and slowly add the olive oil. This will make about 3 cups of Hazelnut Pesto.

MIX chicken with 1 cup of the pesto and the mayonnaise. Use more or less pesto and mayo to suit your taste. Scoop the chicken salad onto your favorite bread for a sandwich or onto a bed of greens for a salad.

Serves 4 – 6

TURKEY SANDWICH

with Cranberry Relish and Chipotle Mayo

This is the best-selling sandwich at The Farm Kitchen, and has been the favorite since we opened in 1993.

Ingredients

2 slices multi-grain bread
2 tablespoons Chipotle Mayo
   (recipe follows)
4 ounces grilled turkey

field greens
2 tablespoons Cranberry Relish
   (recipe follows)

Preparation

SPREAD 1 piece of bread with Chipotle Mayo. Put the turkey and a handful of field greens on the bread. Spread the other piece of bread with Cranberry Relish and put it on top of the greens. Slice the sandwich in half and enjoy.

Serves 1

For the Cranberry Relish

1 pound cranberries
2 cups sugar

1 cup water
2 jalapeños, seeded and chopped

PUT all ingredients in a pan over medium heat. Bring it to a boil, and then simmer until all the berries have popped and the sauce thickens.

Yield: about 3½ cups

For the Chipotle Mayo

2 cups mayonnaise

¼ cup canned chipotle chile purée

MIX the mayonnaise with the chile purée. If it is too spicy, add more mayonnaise. If it is not spicy enough, add more purée.

Yield: about 2¼ cups

Pecan Shortbread Cookies

Ingredients

1 pound butter (4 sticks)
2 cups sugar
2 eggs
4 cups flour

1 teaspoon salt
1½ cups chopped pecans
whole pecans, to garnish
powdered sugar, to garnish

Preparation

HEAT oven to 350 degrees. Cream butter and sugar in a mixer on low speed. Add eggs, one at a time. Add flour and salt slowly and then add chopped pecans. Scoop generous table-spoons of dough onto a cookie sheet and press a whole pecans into the center of each cookie. Bake them for 20 minutes or until the edges are golden brown. Allow the cookies to cool, then roll them in powdered sugar.

Serves 3½ dozen

Chocolate Chip Macaroons

Ingredients

⅔ cup sweetened condensed milk
1½ teaspoons vanilla
1 egg white

⅛ teaspoon salt
3½ cups coconut
1 cup chocolate chips

Preparation

HEAT the oven to 300 degrees. Gently mix together all ingredients until incorporated. Spoon or mound the cookies onto a parchment-lined cookie sheet. Bake for approximately 25 minutes, and then cool on a wire rack.

Serves 15

Nuts From The Farm:
Sugared Pecans, Southwest Nut Mix, and Sweet & Spicy Pecans

Sugared Pecans

1   pound pecan halves
4   tablespoons water

1   cup sugar

HEAT the oven to 300 degrees. Coat pecans with water and toss them with sugar. Spread them onto a parchment-lined cookie sheet. Bake for approximately 15 minutes and let cool for 30 minutes. Store in an airtight container up to 2 weeks.

Yield: about 4 cups

Southwest Nut Mix

3   tablespoons butter
½   pound pecan halves
½   pound macadamia nut halves
½   pound walnut halves

½   cup pumpkin seeds
2   tablespoons kosher salt
2   tablespoons chili powder

MELT the butter in a skillet. Add rest of the ingredients. Cook for approximately 10 – 15 minutes until the nuts are golden brown. Transfer to a brown paper bag for 30 minutes.

Yield: about 6 cups

Sweet & Spicy Pecans

1   pound pecan halves
2   tablespoons cumin
1   tablespoon chili powder

⅛   teaspoon cayenne pepper
    salt to taste
4   tablespoons sugar

BLANCH pecans in boiling water for 2 minutes. Coat lightly with the seasonings, salt, and sugar. Deep-fry them for 3 – 5 minutes in 350-degree oil. Remove from the fryer and toss them in the remaining seasoning. Drain off the excess and cool before serving.

Yield: about 4 cups

TEPARY BEAN HUMMUS
with Garden Vegetable Crudités

The Tepary Bean Hummus makes a great dip for fresh vegetables. Feel free to substitute your favorite bean for Tepary beans. They are native to the Sonoran Desert, and are produced locally in Maricopa, Arizona. They are often available at Farmer's Markets in and around Phoenix.

Ingredients

1 cup Tepary beans, cooked in salted
    water until tender
2 cloves garlic, roasted
2 ounces olive oil

1 tablespoon lemon juice
salt and fresh cracked pepper to taste
assorted fresh vegetables for crudités

Preparation

IN A food processor, purée beans and garlic, and then slowly add in the olive oil. When a smooth consistency is reached, add lemon juice and season it to taste with salt and pepper. The hummus can be adjusted with water or additional olive oil for a creamier purée.

SERVE the hummus with an assortment of vegetables that have been cleaned and cut to bite-size pieces, such as turnips, baby carrots, radishes, beets, tomatoes, and peppers.

Serves 8

CHICKEN LIVER PÂTÉ

Chicken liver makes an excellent pâté that is best served on simple crostini. This classic pâté is popular in Italy as an antipasto.

Ingredients

1 ounce butter
1 ounce olive oil
1 medium onion, diced
2 bay leaves

1 pound chicken livers, cleaned and free
  of membranes
salt and pepper to taste

Preparation

IN A pan over medium heat, combine butter and olive oil. Add onion and bay leaves and sweat onion until translucent. Add chicken livers to the pan and sauté until they are just firm to the touch, about 5 – 6 minutes. Remove the bay leaves. Put the remaining contents of the pan into a food processor and purée until smooth. Season to taste with salt and pepper. To serve, spread on bread, crostini, or crackers.

Serves 4 – 6

GARDEN GREEN SALAD, SPRING ROOTS, AND HERBS

with Lemon Vinaigrette

This salad can be adjusted to include your favorite vegetables. The dressing is refreshing, without overpowering the beautiful flavor of the fresh vegetables.

Ingredients

1 bunch baby carrots
1 bunch Easter egg radishes
1 bunch French radishes
1 bunch Chiogga beets

1 pound local salad greens
4 basil leaves
1 ounce parsley, chopped
Lemon Vinaigrette (recipe follows)

Preparation

SHAVE the carrots, radishes, and beets on a mandolin. Toss them with the greens. Add the basil and parsley and season with salt and pepper. Drizzle the Lemon Vinaigrette over the mix and continue to toss. Plate and serve.

Serves 8

For the Lemon Vinaigrette

4 ounces lemon juice
1 tablespoon shallots, chopped
1 tablespoon garlic, chopped

8 ounces olive oil
2 sprigs oregano
salt and pepper to taste

WHISK lemon juice, shallots, and garlic with the olive oil. Submerge oregano in the dressing, and season with salt and pepper to taste.

Warm Potato, Bacon, and Iitoi Onion Salad

This is a great side dish on its own, or great paired with roasted or grilled chicken. The Iitoi onion is bigger than a green onion, but smaller than a leek. It can be found in some upscale gourmet produce stores and at some farmers markets.

Ingredients

6 large Yukon gold potatoes, cubed and tossed with olive oil
10 strips bacon, diced small
1 carrot, diced small
2 stalks celery, diced small
1 tablespoon garlic, minced

1 tablespoon shallots, minced
1 bunch Iitoi onions, thinly sliced
4 tablespoons whole grain mustard
2 tablespoons sherry vinegar
    salt and pepper to taste

Preparation

HEAT oven to 350 degrees. Season potatoes with salt and pepper to taste and roast them for 30 – 45 minutes. They will be golden brown and tender when done.

IN A large sauté pan over medium heat, fry the diced bacon until it is nearly crisp. Add carrot, celery, garlic, and shallots, and sauté until slightly softened. Add roasted potatoes and toss to combine well. Add Iitoi onions, mustard, and vinegar and sauté until well combined and the onions just start to wilt. Season to taste with salt and pepper and serve warm.

Serves 8

Spinach Linguine

When spinach is in season, it produces a beautiful and flavorful pasta dough. Working with fresh pasta is based a lot on the feel and touch of the dough. Look for your dough to be smooth, not tacky or dry.

Ingredients

4 cups all purpose flour	½ cup spinach, blanched and chopped
5 whole eggs	½ teaspoon salt

Preparation

SIFT flour onto a large worktable. Using your fist, make a well in the center of the flour. Crack the eggs into the well and add spinach and salt. Using a fork, incorporate flour and egg until the mixture becomes thick and pasty. Work the remainder of the flour in with your hands and knead the dough until it is smooth and soft. Allow the dough to rest for 30 minutes covered with plastic.

USING a pasta machine, roll out the dough to the desired thickness. Cut the dough using a linguine cutter. This pasta can be dried or used immediately. Cook the pasta in salted boiling water until al dente, and serve with a favorite sauce or vegetables.

Serves 8

ALMOND CAKE

This is a versatile cake that is great served with fruit, ice cream, or simply whipped cream.

Ingredients

7 ounces butter (15 tablespoons)	¼ pound almonds, finely ground
10 ounces egg whites	¼ pound all purpose flour
¼ teaspoon vanilla	1 teaspoon salt
10 ounces powdered sugar, sifted	1 teaspoon baking powder

Preparation

HEAT oven to 350 degrees. Melt butter until nicely browned and cool slightly. Beat egg whites until soft peaks form, and add vanilla. Combine sugar, almonds, flour, salt, and baking powder and add to the egg white mixture. Slowly stir in the brown butter. Pour the batter into a buttered and floured 12-inch cake pan. Bake for 20 – 25 minutes until the cake is set and golden brown. Serve warm.

Serves 8

The Asylum Restaurant

200 Hill Street
Jerome, AZ 86331
928-639-3197
www.theasylum.biz

Lunch served daily
11:00am to 3:00pm
Dinner served nightly
5:00pm to 9:00pm

The Asylum Restaurant

Richard Pasich, Chef/Co-Owner
Paula Woolsey, Sommelier/Co-Owner
Eric Woolsey & Jennifer Nagel,
Co-Owners

Take time to spend a night in Jerome, a town that has had many names: The Wickedest City in the West, America's Most Vertical City, and the Largest Ghost Town in America. When you come, be sure to visit the historic Jerome Grand Hotel and dine in its lovely restaurant, The Asylum. The five-story Spanish Mission structure was originally built in 1926 to serve as the United Verde Hospital. At the time, Jerome was called the Billion Dollar Copper Camp with a population of 15,000, composed mostly of miners who worked the rich copper claims. The building served as a hospital until the 1950s when it was closed and remained idle until the Altherr family purchased it in 1994 and began restoring the structure to its former glory and to serve as a hotel. Perched on top of 5,200 foot Cleopatra Hill, guests are treated to the breathtaking views of the Verde Valley, including the red rocks of Sedona. The hotel has been named a National Historic Landmark Hotel. Larry Altherr, the owner, describes the hotel as offering the quaintness of a bed and breakfast with the privacy and services of a hotel.

Located in the restored hotel is The Asylum, self-described as "a restaurant on the fringe". Richard and Jennifer along with Eric and Paula, welcome all to a fine dining experience with a relaxed dress code and an emphasis on having fun. The paper and crayons that are provided are not just for kids. The restaurant already has a large collection of art drawn by guests of all ages. Whimsically, reminders of the building's former use are scattered throughout the restaurant in the form of antique wheelchairs and flower-bearing bedpans. The beautiful arched windows frame magnificent sunsets as you order from the menu that features new American cuisine with a southwest flavoring.

Sommelier, Paula Woolsey, has put together an intriguing wine list featuring many "boutique" wineries from around the world. A unique Wine Tasting Menu is available that allows you to choose four two-ounce glasses of wine for a very reasonable price, letting you play winemaker; tasting, comparing, and even blending the choices. Both owners are avid wine enthusiasts, and are proud of the achievement of winning the *Wine Spectator Award of Excellence* every year since 2001. The restaurant has also been awarded the AAA *Three Diamond Award* and has also received the *Wine Enthusiast Award of Distinction*.

 Award of Excellence

The Asylum Restaurant

ROASTED BUTTERNUT SQUASH SOUP

with Cinnamon-Lime Crema

This has been our signature soup from the very beginning. Guests from all over call for this recipe, and it is a favorite for holidays. More than one self-proclaimed squash-hater – after reluctantly and bravely tasting our soup – decided that maybe squash wasn't so bad after all. Be careful of the chilies. Depending on the season, the heat of the individual chili may vary.

Ingredients

1-2 butternut squash (2-3 pounds)
   butter to sauté
1 ounce garlic, minced
⅓ poblano pepper, julienned
1 serrano chili, minced fine
1 small white onion, chopped
3-4 ounces Oak Creek Amber beer, or
   favorite local amber brew
2 cups chicken stock
4 cups water
7 ounces green chiles, diced (frozen will
   work)

2 ounces light brown sugar
⅛ tablespoon cinnamon
1 pinch nutmeg
½ tablespoon salt and pepper, or steak
   salt blend
2 cups heavy cream
   chopped green onions, to garnish
1 ounce Cinnamon-Lime Crema
   (recipe follows)

Preparation

HEAT oven to 400 degrees. Cut the squash in half and remove the seeds. Place the squash in a shallow roasting pan with water and roast until very tender, approximately 45 minutes or more. Remove from the oven and cool. Preheat a stockpot until scorching hot, add a small amount of butter or oil (we like a blend) and sauté the garlic, poblano, Serrano, and onion. Deglaze with beer, and then add the chicken stock and water. Peel squash and add to the pot. Finish with the green chiles, brown sugar, cinnamon, nutmeg, salt, and pepper. Simmer together for 30 minutes. When ready to serve, purée the soup, add the heavy cream and heat gently. Serve with the Cinnamon-Lime Crema (available pre-made in Mexican markets or make it yourself) and chopped green onions.

Serves 8 with 6-ounce portions

Wine suggestion: Paula Woolsey, co-owner and sommelier, likes any red pinot with this soup, like a northern California cool-climate pinot. But for fun, she recommends Borsau Tres Picos Garnacha, Arragon, Spain 2004 vintage. "The fruity full body of a garnacha holds up to the spice and richness of this soup," she adds.

For the Cinnamon-Lime Crema

    1 *cup heavy cream*
    ½ *lime, juice from*   1 *pinch cinnamon*

COMBINE the cream, lime juice, and cinnamon in a mixing bowl and whip until the desired thickness is reached. You may create designs by placing the crema in a squeeze bottle or plastic bag with the corner cut off (like an impromptu pastry bag). We then run a toothpick through the designs to create a "web." Garnish with chopped green onions in the center of your design.

Grilled Sea Bass.

GRILLED SEA BASS
on a Cilantro Potato Pancake with Chardonnay Chili-Lemon Beurre Blanc

Ingredients

1½ pounds sea bass, halibut, or grouper
    oil, to coat
    salt and pepper to taste
2 cups mashed potato (your favorite
    recipe)

2 tablespoons cilantro, minced fine
    fresh watercress and chives, for
    garnish
    Chardonnay Chili-Lemon Beurre Blanc
    (recipe follows)

Preparation

CLEAN and filet the fish, and cut it into 4 equal portions. Brush it with oil, sprinkle with salt and pepper, and set aside. Pre-heat the grill or get the mesquite started.

MAKE the mashed potatoes and mix in the cilantro. Heat a dry, seasoned cast iron skillet to hot (350 degrees), and drop in the mashed potatoes as though making a pancake. Cook until golden brown, then flip and cook the other side until golden brown. Hold in a warm oven until ready to serve.

GRILL the fish to desired doneness. Then stack the individual grilled fish and fresh steamed or grilled vegetables of your choice on each prepared cilantro pancake. Spoon the Chardonnay Chili-Lemon Beurre Blanc on top, sprinkle some around the plate for presentation, and garnish with fresh watercress and chives.

Serves 4

Wine suggestion: "Liquid gold in a glass, aka Selby Russian River Chardonnay 2004," suggests Paula Woolsey, co-owner/sommelier of the Asylum. The subtle butter and mineral flavors of this chardonnay enhance the heat and full flavor of the beurre blanc sauce.

For the Chardonnay Chili-Lemon Beurre Blanc

2 poblano peppers, julienned
½ white onion, julienned
2 serrano peppers, minced
1 tablespoon garlic, minced
12 ounces white wine (same variety that
    you are pairing with the meal)
1 lemon, juice from

8 ounces butter, cold and sliced into 8
    pieces
1 tablespoon chives, minced
1 tablespoon cilantro, minced
1 tablespoon green onions, minced
    salt and pepper to taste

COMBINE the poblano, onion, serrano, and garlic. Blister this mix in an extremely hot, dry sauté pan. Deglaze with the wine and lemon juice and reduce to syrup consistency. Turn off the heat and whisk in the cold butter, bringing the temperature of the hot pan and cold butter together as not to break the sauce. Finish with finely minced, fresh cilantro, chives, and green onions. Add ample amounts of salt and black pepper to taste. Reserve for serving.

Yield: 2 cups

ACHIOTE RUBBED PORK TENDERLOIN
with Chipotle Apricot Glaze

This entrée has been a long-standing favorite among Asylum regulars. Chef Pasich has incorporated local flavors such as apricots, achiote paste, chipotles, pecan honey, and citrus to create a unique southwestern twist. The Chipotle Apricot Glaze recipe makes enough for eight, and I recommend doubling it as it keeps well and is great on toast, a sandwich, or other grilled meats.

Ingredients

2 pounds pork tenderloin
   Achiote Marinade (recipe follows)

1½ cups Chipotle Apricot Glaze
    (recipe follows)

Preparation

ALLOW the pork to marinate in the Achiote Marinade for a minimum of 1 hour. Trim the silver skin and excess fat off the pork tenderloin and cut into 8-ounce portions for grilling. Coat all sides of the tenderloin and let it marinate for 1 hour more. (We often marinate the pork overnight.)

PRE-HEAT the grill, or if you can, use mesquite wood. Grill the meat until medium rare (125 degrees), then let it rest until it warms up to 130 or 135. Be careful not to overcook it or it will be very dry.

MIRROR the Chipotle Apricot Glaze on the plate and cut the portioned pork into 4 straight down cuts. Place the cuts face up on the sauce. Serve with mashed potatoes and fresh vegetables. We top ours with shoestring potatoes, fresh cut chives, and garnish with watercress (another local item).

Serves 4

Wine suggestion: Owner/sommelier Paula Woolsey recommends Seghesio Zinfandel, Sonoma County, 2004 vintage, "a lovely, spicy Zin that works great with this mildly spicy and sweet pork."

For the Achiote Marinade

½ cup salad oil
½ tablespoon achiote paste
¼ orange, juice from
1 tablespoon cilantro, minced

½ tablespoon chili powder, or smoked
   Sonoron spices of your choice
¼ tablespoon salt and pepper, or steak
   salt blend

COMBINE all the marinade ingredients until well blended.

For the Chipotle Apricot Glaze

¼ *pound dried apricots*
¼ *bunch fresh cilantro*
1½ *ounces chipotle pepper in adobo,*
     rinsed and drained
1¼ *cups apri-gel (found at fine pastry*
     stores, or you may substitute with a
     smooth apricot jelly)

3 *ounces pecan or mesquite honey*
1 *ounce cider vinegar*
2 *ounces dark corn syrup*
1 *ounce fresh lime juice*
1 *ounce fresh orange juice*

SLICE the apricots ¼ inch thick lengthwise and reserve. Place the cilantro and drained chipotles in a food processor and blend slightly, just long enough to mince fine (or mince by hand). Set aside. Place the apri-gel, honey, vinegar, corn syrup, lime juice, and orange juice in a mixing bowl and blend until they are smooth. Hand stir in the apricots, cilantro, and chipotles. Allow to settle; this will make the glaze clear.

The Asylum Restaurant

Up the Grand Canyon from Moran's Cove 1903.

Heartline Café

1600 West Highway 89A   Lunch served Daily
Sedona, AZ 86336   11:00am – 3:00pm
928-282-0785   Dinner served Nightly
www.heartlinecafe.com   5:00pm – 9:30pm

Heartline Café

Chuck Cline, Executive Chef, Owner
Phyllis Cline, Owner
Ramon Ruvalcaba, Chef

The story of the Heartline Café is a fairytale story of a dream come true. Chuck originally planned on being a doctor but, like so many soon-to-be-chefs, he got hooked on the culinary life while working in a restaurant during high school. After graduating from the Culinary Institute of America at Hyde Park, he moved around to several positions before settling in as Executive Chef at 40 Main Street Restaurant in Millburn, New Jersey. At the same time, Phyllis was attending Cook College, and taking most vacations in Arizona where her sister, Karen, was attending Arizona State University. She fell in love with the state and vowed to return.

As fate would have it, Phyllis eventually found a job at 40 Main Street Restaurant and the fairytale story began. Brought together by the camaraderie of the kitchen, Chuck and Phyllis would often join the rest of the crew after closing and go to Manhattan to dance. Love took hold and, as they planned their wedding, Phyllis convinced Chuck that the perfect place for a honeymoon was in Sedona at the romantic L'Auberge. Chuck was soon seduced into sharing Phyllis' dream, and the two vowed to return one day to Sedona and run their very own restaurant. They went back to New Jersey, saved their money, and started planning their dream. Several years later, Phyllis met her sister in Sedona to introduce her to her nephew, young Charles Christian. They had lunch at a little restaurant named The Hidden Garden, and Phyllis fell in love with the place; picturing it as the perfect size and structure that they had dreamed of. As a real estate agent, Karen helped them pursue the purchase and, in 1991, Chuck and Phyllis fulfilled their dream with the opening of Heartline Café.

The name of the restaurant was chosen based on the paintings of John Nieto, who featured the Zuni Indian symbol of a bear with numerous Zuni heartlines depicted. When they learned that the symbol represented long life, good health, and good luck, they new they had the perfect name and symbol for their endeavor.

Chuck has created an eclectic menu for the restaurant, which features innovative presentations with touches of Asia, Europe, and the Mediterranean. The cozy interior and garden area serve as a perfect setting for the Clines' motto of "Fine food with a casual mood". The restaurant has won the *Wine Spectator's Award of Excellence* and in 2000, they published an excellent cookbook, *Recipes from Sedona's Heartline Café* that remains very popular.

 Award of Excellence

Pecan-Crusted Trout with Dijon Cream Sauce

Ingredients

1 cup pecans, finely chopped
1 cup unseasoned breadcrumbs
½ teaspoon salt
¼ teaspoon black pepper
½ teaspoon powdered garlic

1 teaspoon fresh thyme, chopped
4 boneless trout, heads removed
1 cup corn oil
Dijon Cream Sauce (recipe follows)

Preparation

MIX pecans, breadcrumbs, salt, pepper, garlic, and thyme in a large bowl. Coat each trout evenly in the mixture. Heat a large sauté pan filled with ½ cup of the corn oil to medium-high heat. Carefully place one crusted trout in the pan, skin side up. Allow the fish to begin to brown, about 2 – 3 minutes. Carefully turn fish over, sprinkle with a pinch of salt and lower heat to medium. Continue to cook for 2 - 3 more minutes, until the flesh is no longer translucent. Repeat with the remaining trout, adding oil as necessary.

AT Heartline, the trout is served on a bed of hot, cooked white rice, brown rice, and wheat berries. Drizzle the top with Dijon Cream Sauce.

Serves 4

Wine suggestion: Savignon Blanc or Fume Blanc, such as Cakebread Cellars

For the Dijon Cream Sauce

½ cup fish or chicken broth
2 tablespoons whole grain mustard

¼ cup cream

IN A small saucepan, bring broth to a gentle simmer. Add mustard, and then cream. Stir and continue to simmer until the sauce thickens. Remove from heat and reserve for serving.

Barbecued Pork with Apple Fig Chutney

Ingredients

12 ounces boneless pork loin	½ cup brown sugar
1 tablespoon achiote paste (optional)	2 12-ounce bottles beer
1 tablespoon garlic, minced	1 small yellow onion, diced
½ teaspoon ground cumin	1 carrot, peeled and diced
½ teaspoon cayenne	1 stalk celery, diced
1½ cups good quality barbecue sauce	Apple Fig Chutney (recipe follows)

Preparation

RUB pork with achiote paste, garlic, cumin, and cayenne and allow to set for 1 hour.

HEAT oven to 300 degrees. In a glass baking dish, mix barbecue sauce, brown sugar, beer, onion, carrot, and celery, and place the pork on top. The vegetables on the bottom will keep the pork from sticking and burning. Cover with foil and bake until done. Cooking time may vary, so start to check for doneness after 1 hour. It is finished when the pork is still moist, but is so tender that it tears easily with a fork. The longer it is cooked, the more tender it becomes. Remove from oven and allow to cool to room temperature. Shred the pork by hand and mix with the ingredients in the roasting dish.

REFRIGERATE until ready for use, or serve immediately on toasted buns, topped with the Apple Fig Chutney.

Serves 3 – 4

Beer suggestion: Oak Creek Gold Lager

For the Apple Fig Chutney

½ cup corn oil	1 cup cider vinegar
1 red apple, peeled, seeded, & diced	1 pinch nutmeg
¼ small red onion, peeled & diced	1 pinch cayenne
½ cup figs, chopped (dried or fresh)	kosher salt and pepper to taste
½ small red pepper, diced	

HEAT corn oil in a medium sized sauté pan over medium heat. Add apple, onion, and figs. Sauté until onions are translucent and then add red pepper, vinegar, and nutmeg. Stir and cook for 10 minutes, until peppers begin to soften. Strain the liquid from the saucepan into a second small pan and set the apple mixture aside. Place the pan with the liquid over medium heat and cook it until the volume has reduced by half. Stir apple mixture back into the reduced liquid and reserve for use. May be refrigerated up to 1 week before use.

GAME TRIO WITH GRILLED POLENTA

Ingredients

¾-1 pound boned, trimmed game (such as buffalo, venison, elk)

¾-1 pound segments game poultry (such as pheasant, quail, or duck)

¾-1 pound other game (such as rabbit, game hen, lamb rack, chops or loin)

2 medium fresh fennel bulbs and leaves, chopped, some leaves reserved for garnish

½ cup whole grain mustard

1 small yellow onion, chopped

½ cup cider vinegar

1 tablespoon juniper berries, crushed

2 tablespoons fresh thyme, chopped

1½ tablespoons garlic and shallots, chopped

1 cup olive oil, divided

1 teaspoon black pepper

⅛ cup gin

⅛ cup Sambuca or Anisette

salt to taste

1 cup duck, beef, or veal stock

Grilled Polenta (recipe follows)

Preparation

PREPARE game meats for marinating and set aside. Purée fennel, mustard, onion, vinegar, juniper berries, thyme, garlic, shallots, and 4 tablespoons of the olive oil. Add pepper, gin, and Sambuca or Anisette and process in a food processor to make a chunky marinade. Immerse the meats in the marinade in a large covered glass bowl or zip-lock plastic bag. Refrigerate for at least 4 hours, but not more than 24 hours.

REMOVE the meats from the marinade and grill over medium flame, or pan-sear on the stovetop while brushing lightly with olive oil and sprinkling with salt. Too high a heat will cause the liquid in the marinade to flare up. Red game meat is best served rare to medium-rare to maintain tenderness and moisture.

REST the 3 different meats around the Grilled Polenta on 4 plates. Garnish with remaining fennel leaves and drizzle with stock.

Serves 6

For the Grilled Polenta

4 cups water

1 teaspoon salt

1 tablespoon butter

½ cup coarse cornmeal (polenta)

olive oil to coat

BRING the water to a low boil. Add the salt and butter. Whisk in the cornmeal and turn the heat to low. Cook for approximately 15 minutes, stirring frequently to avoid lumps. To grill it, smooth polenta onto a buttered sheet pan and refrigerate until cool and firm, about 3 hours. Cut into triangles or circles. Brush with olive oil and grill or pan-sear in a heavy, oiled skillet until crispy.

Wine suggestion: California Pinot Noir, such as Jordan "J"

Army officers and their wives from Fort Grant in 1876.

L'Auberge Restaurant

L'Auberge
de Sedona

301 Lauberge Lane
Sedona, AZ 86336
928-282-1667
www.lauberge.com

Breakfast Monday through Saturday
7:00am – 10:30am
Sunday Brunch 9:00am – 2:00pm
Lunch Monday through Saturday
11:30am – 2:30pm
Dinner Nightly 6:00pm – 9:00pm

L'Auberge Restaurant

Jonathan Gelman, Executive Chef
Maury Kepley, Restaurant Manager
Milford Brinkerhoff, Cellar Master/Sommelier

If a romantic retreat is what you are looking for, L'Auberge de Sedona is the perfect place to kickback, unwind, and recharge your senses. Located in the beautiful red rock country of northern Arizona, the resort comprises eleven wooded acres in Oak Creek Canyon, only a few steps away from the activity of the charming uptown of Sedona. Guests can choose from three distinct settings: creekside and gardenside cottages with woodburning fireplaces and covered porches, the two-story lodge with individually decorated rooms, and the magnificent Creek House, a beautiful four-bedroom house with a private master suite. Condé Nast has named the resort to the *Condé Nast Traveler's Ninth Annual Gold List* as well as listing it on its list of the top 75 hotels in the United States.

In keeping with the luxurious accommodations of the resort, the L'Auberge Restaurant is committed to the enjoyment of fine wines, spirits, and world-class cuisine. Guests entering the restaurant are greeted with the sight of beautifully aged wood floors and a large wood-burning fireplace with a river rock façade. The formal dining room is dressed in soft gold walls with high-backed chairs draped in a lovely fabric featuring green, white, and rust stripes. The tables are under-covered to the floor with similar fabric and topped with crisp white linen cloths. The adjoining porch, which has a more casual décor, features floor to ceiling windows overlooking the outdoor dining terrace and lovely Oak Creek. From April to October, when the weather permits, guests can enjoy their meals on this beautiful flagstone terrace with its landscaped waterfalls and flocks of wild ducks that rest in the waters of the gurgling creek.

Executive Chef, Jonathan Gelman, most recently from the Arizona Biltmore Resort, has over twenty years experience in senior positions with luxury hotels, resorts, and premium winery restaurants. Before his position at the Biltmore, Chef Gelman served as Executive Chef of catering and banquets at Michael's at the Citadel in Scottsdale. And, among several positions he held in California, Chef Gelman served as Executive Chef of Cuvaison Winery.

The accolades for L'Auberge continue, with the restaurant receiving Mobil's *Four Star* and AAA's *Four Diamond* awards every year since 1988. And, the *Wine Spectator* has awarded it the *Best of Award of Excellence* every year since 1992, in keeping with its extensive wine collection. *DiRona* has also recognized the restaurant as a *Distinguished Restaurant of America*.

 Best of Award of Excellence

COLORADO RACK OF LAMB

with Goat Cheese Potato Terrine, Ratatouille, and Lamb Jus

Ingredients

1 Colorado rack of lamb
   fresh cracked black pepper, to taste
   sea salt, to taste
1 pinch micro sage
1 pinch rosemary dust
2 tablespoons lamb jus

1 Goat Cheese Potato Terrine
   (recipe follows)
1 cup Ratatouille (recipe follows)
   micro sage, to garnish
   rosemary dust, to garnish

Preparation

HEAT oven to 350 degrees. Season lamb with cracked pepper and sea salt. Sear it in a very hot skillet for 1 minute and turn over. Cook another minute and remove from the pan. Place it in the oven for 12 minutes.

TO SERVE, place the Goat Cheese Potato Terrine on a warm plate. Remove lamb from the oven and place next to the terrine, and add the warm Ratatouille. Drizzle with lamb jus, and top with the micro sage and rosemary dust.

For the Goat Cheese Potato Terrine

2 small Yukon gold potatoes
4 farm egg yolks
1 cup goat cheese

1 pinch sea salt
   fresh cracked black pepper to taste
¼ cup heavy cream

HEAT oven to 350 degrees. Thinly slice potatoes. Whisk egg yolks, goat cheese, salt, and pepper together. Slowly add cream to the egg mixture while whisking. In a terrine, layer the potatoes with the egg mixture. Bake for 45 minutes and reserve for serving.

For the Ratatouille

1 tablespoon red onion, minced
1 tablespoon red bell pepper, minced
1 tablespoon gold bell pepper, minced
1 tablespoon purple bell pepper, minced
1 tablespoon eggplant, minced
1 tablespoon Portobello mushroom,
   minced

1 tablespoon zucchini, minced
1 tablespoon yellow squash, minced
1 tablespoon garlic, minced
1 tablespoon shallot, minced
1 tablespoon olive oil

IN A heavy-bottomed skillet, sauté all ingredients in the olive oil. Reserve for serving.

Serves 1

Wine suggestion: 2002 Paul Hobbs "Michael Black Vineyard" Merlot, Napa, CA.

SEARED HUDSON VALLEY FOIE GRAS
with Truffled Apple Custard on Brioche

Ingredients

6 ounces Hudson Valley foie gras
   fresh cracked black pepper to season
   sea salt to season
   flour to coat
1 thick slice brioche bread
2 tablespoons Truffled Apple Custard
   (recipe follows)

Poached Apple Slices and Syrup
   (recipe follows)
1 pinch micro thyme, to garnish
1 pinch mushroom dust, to garnish

Preparation

HEAT oven to 350 degrees. Season foie gras with salt and pepper and lightly dust in flour. Sear in a very hot skillet for 1 minute on each side, then remove from the pan and place in oven for 3 minutes. Toast the brioche slice. Layer brioche with the Truffled Apple Custard and Poached Apple Slices and bake for 3 minutes. Remove from oven and top with foie gras. On a warm plate, spread some custard in a semi-circle pattern. Place the layered brioche on one end of the circle of custard. Drizzle it with the apple syrup, top with the thyme and sprinkle with mushroom dust.

For the Truffled Apple Custard

2 cups milk
1 Tahitian vanilla pod, split
2 farm eggs
4 teaspoons sugar

1 pinch sea salt
4 shavings of truffle
1 ounce white truffle oil

SCALD milk and vanilla pod over a bain-marie. Whisk together farm eggs, sugar, and sea salt. Slowly add milk to the egg mixture while whisking and return the egg and milk mixture to the bain-marie. Cook over hot water until the custard coats the back of a spoon, and then remove the vanilla pod. Finish the custard with the shaved truffles and truffle oil. Reserve for serving.

For the Poached Apple Slices and Syrup

3 cups fresh apple juice
1 Tahitian vanilla pod, split
2 whole star anise
1 cinnamon stick

1 whole nutmeg
½ cup sugar
4 Fuji apples, peeled, cored, & sliced

IN A heavy bottom skillet, mix the apple juice, vanilla pod, star anise, cinnamon stick, nutmeg, and sugar. Bring to a boil and then reduce heat to low. Add apple slices and cook for 3 minutes, then remove apples and place in refrigerator. Strain the liquid and reduce over medium heat until it has the consistency of syrup. Reserve for serving.

Serves 3

Wine suggestion: 1994 Zind-Humbrecht, S.G.N., Pinot Gris, Alsace, France

PEPPER CRUSTED AHI TUNA, FINGERLINGS, AND TRUMPET ROYAL MUSHROOMS IN A PORT WINE SYRUP

Lemon citrus dust can be purchased from most specialty stores, or made at home. We take citrus rinds and completely dry them out, then grind into a fine powder.

Ingredients

7 ounces Hawaiian ahi tuna	*½ cup haricot verts*
1 pinch sea salt	*½ tablespoon butter*
fresh cracked black pepper	*1 tablespoon port wine syrup*
2 fingerling potatoes, blanched	*1 pinch micro chives*
½ cup trumpet royal mushrooms	*1 pinch lemon citrus dust*

Preparation

SEASON ahi tuna with sea salt and cracked black pepper and sear it in a very hot skillet for 1 minute on each side and remove from pan. Sauté fingerling potatoes, trumpet mushrooms, and haricot verts in butter.

ON A warm plate, drizzle a little port wine syrup in a semi-circle pattern. Slice the tuna and place it on one end of the syrup. Arrange potatoes, mushrooms, and haricot verts on the opposite end of the plate. Drizzle ahi with the remaining syrup, top with the chives and sprinkle with lemon citrus dust.

Serves 1

Wine suggestion: 1997 Bertagna, "Clos de Perriere", Vougeot, Premier Cru, Burgundy, France.

COCONUT RISOTTO ON MACADAMIA NUT SHORT BREAD
with Pineapple Coulis

Ingredients

20 ounces coconut purée
23 ounces whole milk
3 ounces sugar
2 Tahitian vanilla pods
7 ounces Arborio rice
4 slices kiwi
4 slices pineapple
4 slices starfruit

4 slices wild strawberries
1 pinch micro spearmint
1 pinch coconut dust
2 chocolate cigarettes
2 Macadamia Nut Short Bread Cookies
   (recipe follows)
   Pineapple Coulis (recipe follows)

Preparation

IN A heavy -bottomed skillet, mix coconut purée, milk, sugar, vanilla pods, and rice. Bring to a boil, and turn heat to low. Cook until most of the liquid has been absorbed; remove from heat and transfer to a shallow pan. Place in refrigerator until serving.

TO SERVE, spoon 6 ounces of the chilled risotto onto one of the Macadamia Nut Short Bread Cookies. Layer a slice of kiwi, pineapple, starfruit, and wild strawberry on top, and top the fruit with another short bread cookie. Add another spoonful of the risotto and more fruit slices on top of the first one. On a chilled plate drizzle the Pineapple Coulis and place the assembled cookies in a decorative manner. Top with the micro spearmint and sprinkle with coconut dust. Decorate with the chocolate cigarettes and serve.

Serves 1

Wine suggestion: 1995 Royal Tokaji, "Essencia," Hungary

For the Pineapple Coulis

1 whole pineapple (cleaned and sliced
   into triangles)
1 Tahitian vanilla bean (scraped)

¼ cup sugar
¼ cup butter
1 ounce Bacardi rum

IN A large skillet heat butter and sugar until caramelized. Add pineapple and vanilla to the caramel. Cook until pineapple is tender. Deglaze pan with rum. Remove contents and place on sheet pan for cooling. When cool, move contents to blender and blend until smooth. Strain blended mixture and refrigerate for use.

Yield: 16 ounces

For the Macadamia Nut Short Bread Cookies

40 ounces butter
20 ounces sugar
40 ounces all purpose flour

20 ounces rice flour
1 cup toasted macadamia nuts

HEAT oven to 325 degrees. In a mixing bowl with the paddle attachment, cream butter and sugar until light and fluffy. While mixing, add both flours and mix until a dough consistency is reached. Roll out the dough on a floured marble slab to ⅛-inch thickness and cut into 3-inch circles. Bake for 12 minutes.

Yield: 4 dozen cookies

L'Auberge Restaurant

Home Camp, Grand Canyon circa 1890.

The Cottage Place Restaurant

126 W. Cottage Avenue
Flagstaff, AZ 86001
928-774-8431
www.cottageplace.com

Dinner Tuesday through Sunday
starting at 5:00pm

The Cottage Place Restaurant

Frank Branham, Executive Chef/Owner
Nancy Branham, Owner

The stone, brick, and gable shingled house on the corner of South Humphreys and West Cottage houses a unique restaurant with a loyal following of locals, along with tourists and visitors who understand fine dining. Originally built in 1909, the house is a good example of the "Bungalow" style of architecture common during the early 20th century in Flagstaff. Several families, including a mayor of Flagstaff and a butcher for the prominent Babbitt family, have occupied the comfortable home. In the mid 1950s, John and Theresa Ortiz purchased the property and raised four children there. In the 1960s, Theresa began selling tortillas from the home and before long it became a thriving family business. At the height of the business, they were traveling a thousand miles a week to deliver their products around northern Arizona. In 1980, Ron Freeman talked the family into letting him rent the home and convert it into a restaurant. After extensive remodeling, he opened The Cottage Place Restaurant in 1981.

The charming house offers dining on the glass-enclosed front porch, as well as in the living and dining areas of the old house. A bright, cheery décor featuring whitewashed walls and fireplace is set with soft pink linen tablecloths and comfortable polished wood chairs upholstered with a lovely floral tapestry. The waitstaff is well trained and eager to make guests feel at home. A six-course chef's tasting menu is offered Thursday through Saturday evenings, and offers an optional wine pairing.

In 1994, Frank and Nancy Branham purchased the restaurant from Kurt and Sharley Gottschalk. With a few upgrades the restaurant remains much as it was when Ron Freeman opened it. Chef Branham was born and raised in Georgia, and graduated from Auburn University in Alabama with High Honors. He began his culinary career as an entry-level employee at Timberline Lodge on Mt. Hood, Oregon. Under the tutelage of Executive Chef, Leif Eric Benson, he learned the basics of classical cooking and earned the position of Sous Chef within five years. In 1988 he left Timberline to become the Executive Chef for The Hotel Group at Steamers Restaurant in Portland, Oregon, and in 1990, he transferred to the Woodlands Plaza Hotel in Flagstaff, where he remained until he and Nancy purchased The Cottage Place Restaurant. Chef Branham began accumulating culinary awards beginning in 1988, when he won The *Judge's Award* and an American Culinary Foundation *Gold Medal* at the Portland Culinary Salon.

The restaurant has also been awards *Wine Spectator's Award of Excellence* every year since 1995

Award of Excellence

Dungeness Crab Cakes

with Roasted Corn Sauce

Ingredients

1 pound Dungeness crabmeat, crumbled
  and thoroughly checked for pieces
  of shell
1 celery stalk, diced, about ½ cup
¼ cup red pepper, diced
1 cup corn kernels
1 teaspoon horseradish
1½ teaspoons Dijon mustard
1 tablespoon lemon juice
1 teaspoon lemon zest

2 tablespoons fresh chives, chopped
½ teaspoon salt
¼ teaspoon white pepper
¹⁄₁₆ teaspoon cayenne pepper
2 cups Japanese breadcrumbs, divided
2 whole eggs
½ cup clarified butter
1 quart Roasted Corn Sauce, divided
  (recipe follows)

Preparation

COMBINE crabmeat, celery, red pepper, corn kernels, horseradish, Dijon, lemon juice and zest, chives, salt, pepper, cayenne, ½ cup of the breadcrumbs, ½ cup of the Roasted Corn Sauce, and eggs. Mix thoroughly. Taste and adjust the seasoning. Divide crab mixture into 16 balls, 2 ounces each. Gently form each ball into a round cake about ½ inch thick. Dredge the cakes in the remaining breadcrumbs, gently pressing the cakes to make the crumbs adhere.

HEAT a large skillet over a high flame. Cover the bottom of the skillet with clarified butter. Fry the crab cakes for 2 or 3 minutes per side or until they are golden brown, and then drain them on a paper towel. Heat remaining Roasted Corn Sauce and keep warm.

TO SERVE, ladle ¼ cup of the warm Roasted Corn Sauce on each plate. Serve the crab cakes in a pool of sauce.

For the Roasted Corn Sauce

2 ears fresh corn, shucked &cleaned
1 tablespoon olive oil
½ cup Marsala wine
2 tablespoons shallots, chopped
2 teaspoons salt

¼ teaspoon white pepper
4 cups whipping cream
1 cup water
2 tablespoons butter, melted
4 tablespoons flour

HEAT oven to 350 degrees. Brush corn with olive oil and place on a cookie sheet. Bake for 30 minutes, turning corn as needed. Let corn cool, and then cut the kernels off the cob. Combine the Marsala, shallots, salt, and pepper in a large saucepan. Bring to a boil and reduce by half. Add whipping cream and water and return to a boil. Add corn kernels. Combine butter and flour to make a roux. Whisk the roux into the boiling sauce and simmer for 20 minutes. Purée the sauce, adjust the seasoning, and strain.

Serves 16 appetizer-sized cakes

Wine suggestion: I love a well-balanced Chardonnay with these crab cakes. The buttery richness and crisp finish of Rombauer or Newton Red Label makes a great match.

VELOUTÉ OF WINTER SQUASH

Autumn is the time to celebrate the harvest. An abundance of produce flows into the markets – bright red peppers, crisp golden apples, fresh yellow corn, and brightly colored winter squash. The pumpkin has become a symbol of fall, but it is only one of many delicious varieties of winter squash. Acorn, butternut, Hubbard, and spaghetti squash are readily available. Below is a recipe using winter squash that is a favorite here at The Cottage Place.

Ingredients

1½ pounds butternut squash
½ pound butter, melted, divided
1 onion, diced
⅔ cup flour
1½ quarts chicken stock
3 cups apple juice
½ teaspoon balsamic vinegar
1 teaspoon soy sauce
¼ cup sugar
½ cup cream or milk

1 teaspoon salt
⅛ teaspoon white pepper
½ teaspoon cinnamon
⅛ teaspoon nutmeg
½ teaspoon curry powder
⅛ teaspoon cayenne pepper
1 Granny Smith apple, peeled, cored, and diced
¼ cup toasted almonds

Preparation

HEAT oven to 350 degrees. Split squash in half lengthwise and remove seeds. Brush the inside of the squash with butter and bake for 1 hour or until tender. While the squash is baking, sauté onion in melted butter until translucent. Remove pan from the heat and stir in flour to make a roux. Set aside.

COMBINE chicken stock, apple juice, balsamic vinegar, soy sauce, sugar, cream, salt, pepper, cinnamon, nutmeg, curry, and cayenne in a stockpot and bring to a boil. Add the onion and flour mixture to the boiling stock, stirring constantly with a whisk. Stir until it is smooth, and then simmer for 20 minutes.

REMOVE squash from the oven, let it cool and then remove pulp. Blend it with enough of the soup to purée smoothly. Add purée to the soup and stir. Check the seasoning. Add apples and simmer for 5 minutes. Serve topped with toasted almonds.

Yield: 10 cups

Arizona Cream with Raspberry Purée

This is the famous Cottage Place non-fat dessert. Even though the Cottage Place is not known for low-fat dining, one of our signature desserts is actually fat free. Arizona Cream is a mousse made with non-fat yogurt and skim milk, and then flavored with honey, lemon zest, and nutmeg. I originally created this dessert for an American Heart Association event when I worked in Oregon, so its original name was "Oregon Cream." After we moved to Arizona and renamed it "Arizona Cream" it won first place for a heart-healthy dessert in "The Taste of Flagstaff." It was also featured as part of a national competition where myself and 11 other chefs from around the country created heart-healthy school lunch menus. It is an easy dessert to make, and can be kept for up to a week, so that when you have the urge for something sweet you can indulge without the extra fat calories. Following, you will find the classic rendition that we always serve at the Cottage Place, but you can be creative by changing the flavor of non-fat yogurt you use, the seasoning, and the topping. Have fun!

Ingredients

2 cups nonfat milk
1¼ cups sugar
1½ tablespoons honey
1¼ tablespoons gelatin
2 teaspoons vanilla extract

2 pounds nonfat yogurt
1 lemon, zest and juice from
  nutmeg to taste
  Raspberry Purée (recipe follows)

Preparation

COMBINE milk, sugar, honey, gelatin, and vanilla in a double boiler and heat to 180 degrees. Remove from the heat and allow to cool to 100 degrees. Add milk mixture to yogurt and then add lemon zest and juice, and season with nutmeg. Adjust seasonings to taste. Pour mixture into service glasses. Chill for several hours and cover with plastic wrap until used. Top with Raspberry Purée prior to serving.

Serves 8

For the Raspberry Purée

2 packages frozen raspberries, 12
  ounces each

6 tablespoons sugar

THAW raspberries, and then purée them in a blender. Add sugar and purée again. Strain through a fine strainer to remove the seeds, and reserve for serving.

Geronimo and fellow Apaches.

Josephine's
Modern American Bistro

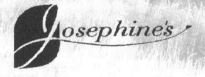

503 N. Humphreys
Flagstaff, AZ 86001
928-779-3400
www.josephinesrestaurant.com

Lunch Monday through Saturday
11:00am – 2:30pm
Dinner Monday through Saturday
5:00pm – 9:00pm

Josephine's Modern American Bistro

Tony Cosentino, Chef/Co-Owner
Jill Cosentino, Co-Owner

Josephine's Modern American Bistro was opened in June 2002 by siblings, Tony and Jill Cosentino. The restaurant was named in honor of their late mother, and is housed in the charming John Milton Clarke home that is listed on the National Historic Register. Several noteworthy Flagstaff families, including the Babitts, have occupied the former home. Constructed in 1911, the building was the first in the area to use malpais, a native volcanic rock. It is a prime example of the utilitarian Craftsman Bungalow style of architecture so prevalent in Flagstaff in the early 20th century. Aspects of this style can be seen in the home's battered rock columns on the expansive porch, the sculpted rafter with diamond sash windows, coffered ceilings, interior French doors, and the extensive use of wainscot paneling in the interior. Today, the building retains much of its original styling and character; surrounding its guests with a graceful and comfortable atmosphere.

Chef Tony has been in the restaurant industry for more than twenty years. Serving as Executive Chef at Forest Highlands for six years, he fully honed his expertise in the culinary arts. The Northern Arizona chapter of the American Culinary Federation awarded him the distinction of *Chef of the Year*, and he has also served as the chapter's president. Jill Cosentino comes from a catering and public relations background and helped to establish the front of the house.

The culinary philosophy of the pair focuses on using local and organic produce whenever available. The menu is frequently updated to showcase the season's best produce and seafood. Chef Tony insists on using only the finest cheeses, such as Maytag blue cheese, Tillamook cheddar, and Parmigiano-Reggiano. No hydrogenated oils or margarine are used on the premise, only extra virgin olive oil and real butter. The menu is considered "Modern American", in that it reflects an eclectic mixture of ethnic cuisines, with flavors of the southwest.

Along with a full bar with excellent cocktails, martinis, and an extensive beer list, Josephine's has a fine wine list that is continuously updated to fully complement the changing menu. In 2005, the *Wine Spectator* magazine recognized the restaurant with its *Award of Excellence*. It has also been awarded AAA's *Three Diamond Award*, and was voted *Best New Restaurant* by the *Market Survey's of America*. The Cosentinos' recipe for success is based on using the finest quality foods, a wonderful and relaxing atmosphere, and excellent service

 Award of Excellence

CHARRED TOMATO JALAPEÑO SALSA

This is one of the chef's favorite condiments. Everyone in the kitchen loves to add this flavorful zesty salsa to a meal. If you are having an outdoor BBQ, this is great with any grilled meats. Get the salsa going first and it will be all ready when your steaks are done.

Ingredients

10 tomatoes, rough chopped	¼ cup ground cumin
3 jalapeños, halved	½ cup ancho chile powder
½ cup whole cloves garlic	½ cup fresh lime juice
½ cup shallots, rough chopped	2 cups V8 or tomato juice
2 red onions, rough chopped	1 bunch cilantro, stemmed
½ cup canola oil	salt and pepper to taste

Preparation

PREHEAT char broiler on high. Mix together tomatoes, jalapeños, garlic, shallots, onions, oil, cumin, and chile powder. Toss them on the grill, being careful not to pour any excess oil directly on the grill, starting a fire. Let it char and turn them over several times. Once there is a good amount of char on your vegetables, put them back in the mixing bowl and add lime juice, V8, and cilantro. Purée in a food processor, then add salt and pepper to taste.

Yield: 1½ quarts

Wine Sugestion: Marquis Philips Shiraz

Roasted Poblano Butternut Squash Soup

Here is one of Josephine's favorite soup recipes. It's a hearty, stick-to-your-ribs, scrum-deli-cious soup. On top of that, it is also healthy. It can be easily converted to a vegetarian recipe by using a vegetable stock instead of chicken stock. It can also be easily converted to a vegan recipe by just leaving the cream cheese out. It is not a lot of cream cheese, but it does add a little richness to the soup.

Ingredients

1 large butternut squash
1 tablespoon garlic, minced
1 large yellow onion, diced
2 teaspoons rosemary, minced
2 teaspoons ginger, minced
1 teaspoon dried basil
1 tablespoon butter or cooking oil
3 cups chicken broth

2 poblano chiles, roasted & peeled
4 ounces cream cheese
1 pinch nutmeg
  salt and pepper to taste
  lime wedge, to finish
  green onion, to garnish
  toasted pumpkin seeds, to garnish

Preparation

HEAT oven to 375 degrees. Cut butternut squash in half lengthwise and scoop out the seeds. Place halves down on a sheet pan with a cup of water and bake until it is soft to the touch, about ½ hour. When it is cool enough to handle, scoop the squash out of the skin.

SAUTÉ garlic, onion, rosemary, ginger, and basil in a little oil until soft. Add chicken stock and bring to a boil. Add roasted squash, poblano, and cream cheese. Purée with either a vertical mixer or food processor. Add the salt and nutmeg. Just before serving, squeeze a little bit of lime over the soup. The fresh acidity brightens up all the flavors. Garnish with scallions and pumpkin seeds if desired.

Yield: 1½ quarts

Wine Suggestion: Genesis Hogue Merlot

Lamb Pine Nut Meat Loaf

We serve this meat loaf both at dinner with mashed potatoes and at lunch as a sandwich. Although it is a fairly simple recipe, it is probably one of my most requested. What makes the difference with this recipe is having good quality ground lamb. We use fresh leg of lamb and grind it ourselves. You may find a butcher shop willing to do this for you.

Ingredients

2 pounds leg of lamb, twice medium ground
1 pound pork, twice medium ground
1 red bell pepper, medium dice
1 large yellow onion, medium dice
6 eggs
2½ cups breadcrumbs

½ pound pine nuts
¾ cup A-1 sauce
½ tablespoon Tabasco
1 tablespoon Worcestershire sauce
2 tablespoons salt
1 teaspoon pepper

Preparation

HEAT oven to 350 degrees. Mix together all of the ingredients. Place in 2 parchment paper lined loaf pans and bake for 45 minutes to 1 hour.

Yield: 2 loaves, 2 pounds each

Wine Suggestion: Consentino Sangiouese

ESPRESSO ANGLAISE

This is great served over our Chocolate Molten Cake.

Ingredients

2 cups half and half
1 teaspoon vanilla extract
1 shot of espresso, or some powdered
   espresso

2 tablespoons Kahlua
4 egg yolks
¾ cup sugar

Preparation

BRING half and half, vanilla, espresso, and Kahlua to a simmer in a heavy-bottomed saucepan. In a separate bowl, mix together egg yolks and sugar. Temper the half and half mixture into the egg mixture by slowly whisking ⅓ of it into the eggs. Now whisk all of the egg mixture back into the saucepan and continue to heat on low to medium heat. Continue to whisk as it thickens. Strain through a fine strainer and let cool for serving.

Yield: 2 cups

Chocolate Molten Cake

This is for hard-core chocoholics only. At Josephine's, we use only Belgium chocolate. Being a chocoholic myself, I do not waste my time with lesser quality chocolates.

Ingredients

8 ounces milk chocolate	4 whole eggs
¾ cup heavy cream	½ tablespoon vanilla extract
12 ounces semi-sweet chocolate	1¼ cup all purpose flour
8 ounces butter	¾ cup unsweetened cocoa powder
¾ cup sugar	½ teaspoon baking soda
3 egg yolks	½ teaspoon salt

Preparation

HEAT oven to 350 degrees. Melt milk chocolate with cream in a double boiler on medium heat, and then chill to firm it up. Melt semi-sweet chocolate and butter in a double boiler. Cream sugar into semi-sweet chocolate mixture. Add yolks, whole eggs, and vanilla and mix, being careful not to over mix. Sift flour, cocoa powder, baking soda, and salt together and add it to the semi-sweet chocolate mixture.

PORTION about 4 ounces of this chocolate cake mixture into cup cake tins. Bake in the oven for 8 – 10 minutes. Once the tops of the cupcakes start to crack slightly from cooking, push a couple of tablespoons of the chilled milk chocolate mixture into the middle of the cake. Cook for 2 more minutes. Let them cool down a little so you can get them out of the tins, then reheat them in the microwave for a few seconds. We serve them with raspberry sauce and espresso anglaise.

Serves 12

Wine Suggestion: Sebastiani Cabernet Sauvignon

GLOSSARY

al dente Italian for "to the tooth", describing pasta or other food cooked only until it offers a slight resistance when bitten into, but which is not soft or overdone.

amuse bouche French, meaning "to amuse the mouth", this is usually a small bit of food before the meal to waken the taste buds.

baste To spoon liquid over food as it cooks, usually fat or drippings, which keeps the food moist.

blanch To plunge food (usually vegetables or fruits) into boiling water briefly, then into cold water to stop the cooking process.

bouquet garnis A bundle of herbs, usually in a cheesecloth sack tied with string, used to flavor dishes and then removed before serving.

brioche A French pastry bread made rich with butter and eggs that is used not only for desserts, but also in many meat and cheese dishes.

brunoise A mixture of vegetables that have been finely diced or shredded, then cooked slowly in butter.

chervil An herb, originally from Asia, with a delicate flavor.

chiffonade Similar to julienne, the process of cutting lettuce, endive, or herbs into thin even strips.

chinois A very fine mesh cone-shaped metal sieve used for puréeing or straining. Often a spoon or pestle is used to press the food through it.

clarify The process of clearing a cloudy substance, such as in stocks or wines, or of melting butter until the foam rises and is skimmed off.

concassé; concassee A French term for chopping or pounding, often applied to tomatoes or herb mixtures.

coulis A general term meaning a thick purée or sauce.

deglaze To add liquid, usually wine or stock, to the skillet to loosen browned bits of food left from sautéing or browning.

demi-glace A rich brown sauce (usually meat stock) combined with Madeira or sherry and slowly cooked until it's reduced by at least half, to a thick glaze.

duxelles A garnish or flavoring made of finely chopped mushrooms, shallots, and herbs sautéed in butter.

emulsify To blend together 2 or more liquids that do not naturally blend, such as oil and vinegar. Done by whisking the ingredients together with an emulsifier such as an egg yolk or milk.

foie gras A gourmet food product usually made from the liver of geese or ducks that have been force-fed and not allowed to exercise. The liver is then soaked overnight, marinated in wine or brandy and then baked.

guanciale Northern Italian in origin. It is made from the cheek and jowls of the hog, instead of the belly. It has a more delicate texture and stronger flavor than pancetta.

julienne A method of cutting vegetables into thin strips, usually about 1 inch by 1/16 inch.

kosher salt	An additive-free coarse-grained salt.
mirepoix; *mirepois*	A mixture of diced carrots, onion, celery, and herbs that is sautéed in butter.
mirin	A sweet, rice wine used in cooking to sweeten meat or fish dishes.
mole	A smooth, cooked blend of onion, garlic, chiles, ground pumpkin or sesame seeds, and a small amount of Mexican chocolate.
nappe	A term indicating the thickness of a liquid, usually described as thick enough to coat the back of a spoon.
pancetta	Slightly salty Italian bacon cured with salt and spices, but not smoked.
panko	Coarse Japanese bread crumbs used for coating fried foods.
pepicha	Also spelled pipicha, an herb similar in taste to a strong cilantro.
Plugrá	A brand of European butter that is richer in fat and has less water content than regular butter. It works especially well when making pastries.
prosciutto	Italian word for ham that is seasoned, salt-cured, air-dried, but not smoked.
quenelle	A light dumpling made of minced or ground fish, meat, or vegetables, seasoned and bound with eggs. The mixture is formed into small ovals and gently poached in stock.
queso fresco	A fresh, white Mexican cheese with a texture similar to farmer's cheese.
reduce; reduction	To boil a liquid rapidly, reducing it until it is thickened. The flavor becomes more intense.
rondeau	A straight-sided, round, shallow pan with a lid and two handles.
roux	A mixture of equal parts flour and butter used to thicken sauces. Cooking different lengths of time results in different flavors and colors.
sambal oelek	A condiment popular in Indonesia and southern India, it is usually made with chiles, brown sugar, and salt. It usually accompanies rice and curried dishes.
sauté	To quickly cook food over direct heat in a small amount of hot oil.
sear	To quickly brown the outside of meat in a hot oven or a hot fry pan. This seals in the juices in preparation for further cooking.
silver skin	A thin, tough, membrane found on meat that will cause the meat to curl when cooked if not removed.
slurry	A thin paste of water and flour used as a thickener.
sweat	To cook vegetables slowly in a tightly covered pan so that they literally stew in their own juice.
tapenade	A spread or condiment, usually consisting of puréed capers, olives, anchovies, & olive oil.
tian	A French term for a shallow earthenware casserole.
truffle	A fungus that is cultivated primarily in France and Italy, valued for its earthy, aromatic nature.
wasabi	Sometimes called Japanese horseradish, this green-colored condiment comes in paste and powder form.

CULINARY SOURCES

This list is provided for your convenience. While many of the suggested suppliers have been recommended, not all suppliers have been individually checked out. We do not endorse any particular vendor or supplier.

BROKEN ARROW RANCH
Antelope, venison, wild boar, sausages
Ingram, TX
800-962-4263
www.brokenarrowranch.com

EARTHY DELIGHTS
Gourmet foods, including fiddlehead ferns
1161 E. Clark Rd, Suite 260
DeWitt, MI 48820
800-367-4709
www.earthy.com

EPICURIOUS
Comprehensive website for recipes and culinary definitions
www.epicurious.com

ETHNIC FOODS
Source for researching and purchasing many foods from around the world.
www.ethnicfoods.com

ETHNIC GROCER WORLD MARKET
Gourmet foods including sriracha (hot chili) sauce
www.ethnicgrocer.com

GOURMET SLEUTH CULINARY SHOP
Gourmet foods, including agave nectar
408-354-8281
www.gourmetsleuth.com

HUDSON VALLEY FOIE GRAS
Foie gras and duck products
80 Brooks Rd
Ferndale, NY 12734
845-292-2500
www.hudsonvalleyfoiegras.com

LOCAL HARVEST
Locate food sources by state
www.localharvest.org

IGOURMET.COM
Gourmet foods, including guajillo powder & quince paste
877-446-8753
www.igourmet.com

INDIAN FOODS COMPANY
Indian foods and recipes, source for channa dal.
www.indianfoodsco.com

KELLER'S CREAMERY
Plugrá butter, sold through Trader Joe's and Whole Foods
855 Maple Ave
Harleysville PA 19438
800-535-5371
www.kellerscreamery.com

NATIVE SEEDS/SEARCH
Whole chiles, chili powder, beans, salsas, corn products
www.nativeseeds.org

PENZEY'S SPICES
Spices, herbs, and seasonings
800-741-7787
www.penzeys.com

QUEEN CREEK OLIVE MILL
Queen Creek olive oil and other products
www.queencreekolivemill.com

SNAKE RIVER FARMS
Kobe beef and Kurobuta pork
Boise, ID
www.snakeriverfarms.com

SWEET CACTUS FARMS
Certified organic agave nectar.
10317 Washington Blvd.
Los Angeles, CA 90232
Phone: 310-733-4343
www.sweetcactusfarms.com

Photo Copyrights/Credits

Front Cover, left to right: ©Janos/J Bar; ©iStockphoto.com/Eric Foltz; ©Pastiche Modern Eatery; ©Kai Restaurant; ©Wildflower; ©Sedona Heritage Museum; ©Arizona Historical Society/Tucson, 46775; ©Terra Cotta; ©elements; ©Kai Restaurant; ©Arizona Historical Society/Tucson, PC171.f7.B; ©Razz's Restaurant

Back Cover, left to right: ©Terra Cotta; ©El Charro Café; ©Jonathan's Cork; ©LON's at the Hermosa; ©Michael's at the Citadel; ©Janos/J Bar

All interior photos: ©Blanche T. Johnson or as noted below.

i: ©Arizona Historical Society/Tucson, 8016; **viii:** ©Arizona Historical Society/Tucson, 63544; **xiv (top):** ©Arizona Historical Society/Tucson, 1447; **xiv (bottom):** ©Arizona Historical Society/Tucson, 61266; **2:** ©Acacia at St. Philips; **7-9:** ©Anthony's in the Citadel; **14:** ©Bistro Zin; **19, 20:** ©El Charro Café; **28:** ©Fuego Restaurant; **33, 34:** ©The Grill at Hacienda del Sol; **41-43, 50, 54:** ©Janos/J Bar; **55, 56, 61:** ©Jonathan's Cork; **63, 64, 67:** ©Pastiche Modern Eatery; **68:** ©Arizona Historical Society/Tucson, B203831; **75-80:** ©Terra Cotta; **81, 82, 87:** ©Wildflower; **88:** ©Arizona Historical Society/Tucson, 530; **89, 90, 93, 95:** ©Kai Restaurant; **97, 98, 102:** ©Bloom; **103, 104, 107, 110:** ©Michael's at the Citadel; **112:** ©Mosiac Restaurant; **122:** ©Arizona Historical Society/Tucson, 10179; **123, 124:** ©North; **128:** ©Arizona Historical Society/Tucson, 26039; **129, 130:** ©Razz's Restaurant; **133-136, 139:** ©Sassi Ristorante; **140:** ©Arizona Historical Society/Tucson, 62152; **142, 145, 147:** ©elements; **148:** ©Arizona Historical Society/Tucson, 46775; **149, 150, 156:** ©LON's at the Hermosa; **157, 158, 160:** ©Christopher's Fermier Brasserie; **163-180:** ©The Farm at South Mountain; **181, 182, 184, 187:** ©The Asylum Restaurant; **188:** ©Arizona Historical Society/Tucson, 25746; **189, 190:** ©Heartline Café/Steve Hansen; **194:** ©Arizona Historical Society/Tucson, 45297; **195, 196:** ©L'Auberge Restaurant; **202:** ©Arizona Historical Society/Tucson, 16009; **204:** ©The Cottage Place; **208:** ©Arizona Historical Society/Tucson, 78162; **210, 211:** ©Josephine's Modern American Bistro

ABOUT THE PUBLISHERS

Chuck and Blanche started Wilderness Adventures Press, Inc. in 1993, publishing outdoor and sporting books. Along with hunting and fishing, they love fine dining, good wines, and traveling. They have always been able to "sniff out" the most outstanding and interesting restaurants in any city they visit.

On weekends, they experiment in the kitchen, cooking a variety of fish and meats, as well as preparing the harvest from their time in the field. This love of cooking has resulted in a large library of cookbooks, and has inspired them to create a series of cookbooks based on their love of travel and fine dining.

Chuck and Blanche make their home in Gallatin Gateway, Montana, along with their four German wirehaired pointers.

INDEX